Crystal Clear

CRYSTAL CLEAR

THE INSPIRING STORY OF HOW
AN OLYMPIC ATHLETE LOST HIS LEGS
DUE TO CRYSTAL METH AND FOUND
A BETTER LIFE

Eric Le Marque

with

Davin Seay

Delacorte Press

Dedicated to my adoring, amazing wife, Hope.
You saved my life and brought harmony and balance into it.
I love you more than the world! For every part of who you are
and for all of the tender loving-kindness you provide to me and
our children. You are a magnificent mother. You are more
than a blessing; you are my HOPE! You are my "SHMILY"!

Proverbs 12.4: An excellent wife is the crown of her husband.

*Proverbs 18.22: He who finds a wife finds a good thing,
and obtains favor from the LORD.*

What follows is a true story. The names of certain characters,
and certain identifying details, have been changed
in order to protect their privacy.

CRYSTAL CLEAR
A Delacorte Press Book / May 2009

Copyright © 2009 by Eric Le Marque
All rights reserved

Published in the United States by Delacorte Press,
an imprint of The Random House Publishing Group,
a division of Random House, Inc., New York

Delacorte Press is a registered trademark of Random House, Inc.,
and the colophon is a trademark of Random House, Inc.

ISBN 978-0-553-80765-3

Printed in the United States of America on acid-free paper

www.bantamdell.com

BVG   9 8 7 6 5 4 3 2 1

First Edition

Book design by Glen M. Edelstein
Title page photo by Davit Barber Productions

Prologue

I RAN BLINDLY, stumbling and falling, pushing my way through chest-high snow. My heart pounded against my ribs and I pulled each breath from the thin freezing air as if it were my last. I could hear the creatures behind me, moving in closer, fanning out to attack from all sides, a pack on the hunt for human prey.

Whimpering with fear, I shouted into the pitch-black wilderness, my desperate voice echoing into the invisible distance.

"No!"

It was a cry of both defiance and utter and abject defeat. I was helpless against the beasts lunging toward me. I couldn't believe I was about to die. It was a vivid, harrowing nightmare and I couldn't wake up. I screamed again, but this time it was nothing more than an anguished, inarticulate cry. I had been reduced to the level of the animals that were going to eat me. All thought and reason had vanished. I was a piece of meat, easy prey for the savage stalkers.

I stumbled, plunging face-first into a deep drift. I struggled to get up, moving just a few feet before I got bogged down again and had to start pushing myself through the snow one laborious step at a time until I finally came to a complete halt. My legs were trembling and I could feel the soaking trickle of the wet snow mingling with my sweat. Terror had paralyzed me. I couldn't move. This was where it would end, in a flurry of sharp teeth and slavering jaws. As I lay motionless, waiting for death, one thought, one question, went round in my brain in an ever-tightening circle:

How did I get here?

The answer was simple.

I was *addicted* to powder.

WHEN I SAY "powder," you might be thinking cocaine, or maybe heroin. But what I'm talking about is even worse: methamphetamine—speed—one of the most dangerous and destructive drugs known to humanity.

For over a year, at a key juncture in my life, my world revolved around little plastic bags of sparkling white crystals. I loved the way meth made me feel, the crystallizing focus and energy and sense of unlimited power that came with that chemical rush, every time I snorted a shimmering line.

In that way, I guess I wasn't much different from the most ravaged speed freak you might see tweaking on the street, talking to himself, obsessing over ever more minuscule details, endowed with a sense of his own importance and omnipotence. I was a crank addict like every crank addict, and I was heading down the same path of death and decay.

Of course, you couldn't tell me that. I was never going to become one of those hollow-eyed, bleeding-gum human wrecks that haunt the underworld of the drug culture. I had too much self-respect for that, too much pride in my physical abilities, and too much confidence in my own willpower. No white powder was ever going to overcome my steely self-control.

Until it did.

But the story of my addiction doesn't stop there. There was another powder I was addicted to, and in a way that addiction was far more potent and seductive than my need for speed had ever been.

That powder came out of the sky, when weather conditions were just right and the freezing bite of the air brought down a dust so fine and pure you could blow it away with a puff of your breath. It covered everything, coating mountains and valleys and the slopes in between until it was all you could see, glinting in the sun or spreading out under a low bank of clouds where earth met heaven.

And it *was* heavenly, in a way that's impossible to

describe to anyone who hasn't launched themselves on a snowboard into that clean, empty space where the only sound is the soft whisper of acceleration and all you're conscious of is a weightless, floating, and buoyant exhilaration.

I was addicted to powdered snow. The crystals are tiny and dry and lighter than air, the polar opposite of the fat, wet, and heavy snow that turns to slush at times as you maneuver through it. Fresh powder gets thrown up in shimmering sheets as you make effortless turns and cutbacks across the crest of a mountain in those precious few hours just after a storm. Your board glides over it with frictionless ease, nothing holding you down and nothing holding you back. Every sensation is heightened, every second stretches to eternity. You feel the flow beneath you, sliding past gravity in a vast white landscape, listening to yourself breathe or holding your breath as you hit a jump and suddenly you're airborne. The wind fills your lungs and the ecstasy of perfection overcomes you.

There's the rush of speed that comes from meth. And then there's the rush of speed that comes from supercharging your senses in fresh powder. There's no comparison. But then again, I didn't have to choose. I was addicted to both of them and in my mind they were intertwined. I lived for powder in one form or another. And before I could shake free of those twin addictions, I had to nearly die. Now an unequivocal shame.

This is the story of that near-death experience,

through the valley of the shadow of death and out the other side. It's a story of addiction, but it's more than that. It's also about how you sometimes have to lose part of yourself, maybe even the part you love the most, before you can really know what makes you whole. It's a story about how finding your strength can come from reaching the limits of your endurance. About finding out that if you never quit, you will always win. It's about God and the unknowable, unimaginable plan God has for our lives.

There was a time when I had no idea what that plan was. There was a time when I begged God to change His plan. And, thankfully, there was a time when I finally surrendered to His plan. They are all part of this story, and one could not have happened without the others.

UNTIL I SURVIVED an ordeal that would strip away every false assumption and easy belief I ever had, I thought I knew who I was. And as far back as I can remember, a big part of that identity was my feet.

That may sound weird. If most people were asked to single out their most important asset, they usually talk about their character and integrity; their mind or their heart or even their face. But for me, it was my feet. They carried me to victory after victory in my life, racking up one achievement after another. My footwork was what had earned me a place on the Boston Bruins lineup in the National Hockey League, the thrill of being selected for three World Championships and the opportunity to play in the 1994 Winter Olympics in Lillehammer. Everything I accomplished as an athlete—and I accomplished a lot from a very young age—involved my feet in one way or another. Even on the slopes, as an expert rider, it was my feet that conveyed to me the sensations of soaring, gliding, floating, and jumping. They allowed me to master the terrain I was negotiating on every run, to make the split-second adjustments and last-minute decisions that gave snowboarding its instinctive and spontaneous thrill. They were what kept me grounded and allowed me to fly.

Like most of us, I took my body, and all its parts, for granted. I expected it to be there when I needed it and perform as required. But it's also true that my personal performance standards were very high. The fact is that my physical abilities, the athletic ability I was born with, defined who I was, to myself and to others. It seemed that I had a knack for anything I tried, starting with skating and hockey, up through baseball, basketball, football, surfing, even golf. And, of course, snowboarding—riding—which was a sport I excelled in above all others. With all of them, it was my feet that led the way to some of the most triumphant, memorable, and exciting moments of my life.

I never imagined what that life might be like without my feet. Who could? The only time you may notice your feet is when they get sweaty or smelly or dog-tired. You flex your ankles and wiggle your toes without thinking about it. They are an extension of us, the way we get around in this world, and without them the horizons of that world can shrink to nothing.

That's what happened to me. I lost my feet, my legs were cut off eight inches below the knee, and my world was suddenly reduced to the four walls of a hospital room. Through a combination of overconfidence and poor judgment, brought on by my meth addiction, I allowed my feet to freeze. Even as I realized what was happening, I did everything I could to reverse the process. But it was too late. The parts of my body that had taken me so far, so fast, were dead. And if they weren't cut away from me, I would have died also. For once in my life, I had no choice. But that didn't make the decision any easier. I'd be lying if I said that there haven't been times since, in my darkest hours, when I regretted that decision, times when death seemed preferable to what I had to endure.

BUT THERE WAS a time when I would have traded everything for a pair of thick dry socks or a cup of hot soup. Late in the afternoon of February 6, 2004, I was getting ready for my last run of the day down Mammoth Mountain in California's Sierra Nevada range. I had purposely moved off the main trails in search of the fresh powder recently dumped by a big winter storm and not yet traversed by the hordes of skiers and snowboarders who flock to the slopes every season. I found what I was looking for in a remote area called Dragon's Back, where I delved off a big hit, a steep drop, at "Beyond the Edge," a trail on the eastern-most flank of Mammoth Mountain.

I'd packed light that day, expecting to be back, soaking in the hot tub of the condo I had borrowed, just as night fell. I had a ski jacket and pants with the linings removed to maximize my maneuverability, and in my pockets I carried four pieces of Bazooka bubble gum, a cell phone with a dying battery, my MP3 player, a twenty-dollar bill, the key to the condo, and a small plastic Ziploc bag with about a half gram of speed.

As I stood on the spine of Beyond the Edge, scoping out the territory, I glanced east to see a solid wall of storm clouds heading my way. It was engulfing everything, consuming the vast range around me in angry gray clouds. Judging from its speed and intensity, I knew it would overtake me in a matter of minutes. No problem. That was just enough time for one final run. . . .

Eight days later, a National Guard Black Hawk helicopter dropped a rescue harness onto the snowbound summit slope of the mountain to pull me to safety. My body temperature was eighty-six degrees. I had lost forty pounds. I had eaten nothing but cedar bark, foliage, and pine seeds for over a week. I had endured nighttime wind-chill factors of twenty below. I was stalked by wolves, slept in snowfields with no shelter, fell into a raging river and was nearly swept over an eighty-foot waterfall. I had survived in those conditions longer than anybody else on record. They called me the Miracle Man.

They don't know the half of it.

I've said that this isn't just another addiction story. But it's not just a survival story, either. In one way, what happened to me up on that mountain was totally unexpected. I was thrown into the middle of a do-or-die situation, unprepared for nature at her most unforgiving. I had been using meth for months, and even though I knew what it was doing to me, I wasn't quite ready to quit. As a result, I had compromised my objectivity and my ability to make sound decisions, not to mention my physical stamina. No one was more surprised than me to find out that I had put myself in a life-threatening situation. I was too experienced, too much of a pro to find myself this vulnerable and exposed.

But from another perspective, my whole life had been preparation for the trial I went through on that mountain. It wasn't just my aptitude for sports—the physical conditioning and mental attitude I had painstakingly developed over the years. It was an innate toughness, a determination to persevere, and the ability to push myself to the limit that got me through. I learned those things from some of the most important people in my life, people like my granddad and my stepfather. They demanded a lot from me, and in turn, I demanded a lot from myself. God's plans may be mysterious, but I believe that He never gives you more than you can handle. I had learned to handle a lot.

During those eight days I ranged between extremes of

hope and despair; expectation and disappointment; fear and courage; and, finally, faith. The physical tribulations that I endured were matched by the emotional highs and lows that swept over me from day to day and even hour to hour. As I was withdrawing from one kind of powder— meth—I was learning a whole new respect for the other kind of powder—the snow that I struggled through, sometimes waist-deep, sometimes chest-deep. I fought for my life to the extreme limits of my own strength.

As you've probably guessed by now, my whole story is one of extremes. I had lived my life purposely pushing the envelope until I finally pushed through. Those eight days on the mountain proved to me that my will to live was stronger than the reckless drive that fed my addictions. I was faced with elemental forces that overpowered me. But in my helplessness I discovered another kind of strength. My fight for survival may have ended when that giant Black Hawk chopper appeared over the top of the ridge like an angel of deliverance. But I was just beginning the biggest struggle of my life.

It's only in those opposites, those extremes, that I can begin to make sense of what happened to me. My addictions to powder, to speed, and to snow, were symptoms of a life out of balance. What replaced them—an incredible wife and beautiful family—are the down payments on a future I never imagined could be mine.

But I'm not there yet. The price I paid for the lessons I've learned has been steep. Adjusting to life without my feet, to performing the daily tasks that we all take for granted, has been, in its own way, every bit as challenging as the eight days I spent lost in the frozen wilderness. I'm reminded of that every time I have to crawl on my hands and knees to the toilet in the middle of the night.

I've heard that there are separate stages to the process of dying: denial, anger, bargaining, acceptance, etc. I've gone through most of those stages as I've experienced the death of the life I used to live and the boy I used to be. It hasn't been easy and on more than a few days the most urgent question I ask myself, God, or anyone else who will listen is: why me?

But on the other side of that extreme is the fact that I still don't think of myself as handicapped. I believe that a big part of the reason why all this has happened is so that I can prove to myself and to others that we can overcome anything with the right attitude, the right combination of determination and humility along with a solid faith.

That's why I'm writing this book. I want to inspire people. I want to motivate them. I want them to know there is no obstacle in their life that can't be overcome. At the same time, I want readers, especially young readers, to take a close look at the wrong turns I've made in my life and learn from them, too. My hope is that I can keep others from making some of the same mistakes I made, while at the same time encouraging them to reach for their dreams.

That's a lot to accomplish in a couple of hundred

pages. But I feel as if I've already accomplished a lot, just by getting to a place where I can tell the story of my life so far. As much as I want to touch anyone who picks up this book, writing it down is also a way for me to put it all in perspective, to get a glimpse of the big picture and pass along the lessons I've learned.

I'm not addicted to powder anymore. I don't do meth or any other drug, including painkillers, and even though I still enjoy the occasional snowboard run with my wife and family, it's no longer an obsession. I can enjoy it for what it is — a way to appreciate the glory of God's creation. These days, when I'm out on the slopes, I take a minute to remember what it was like during those eight dark days. That's when I realize the truth behind the old saying: what doesn't kill you makes you stronger.

CHAPTER ONE

Fresh Tracks

I GOT UP late that morning. It was close to ten when I opened my eyes, to the sound of some wild animal fishing in the garbage cans. As soon as I realized what time it was, I could only think about one thing: the mountain was already open and I wasn't out there capping it.

My feeling of frustration grew when I glanced out the window and saw that, after five days of a heavy blizzard and thick fog, the sky was now a bright and cloudless blue. The storm that had brought me up to Mammoth Mountain a week earlier had passed. The weather report had called for five to seven feet. Instead, almost fifteen feet of fresh champagne powder had been dumped. Conditions were going to be epic. This is what I lived for.

Of course, so did a lot of other guys. As I jumped out of bed and quickly began getting myself ready for a day of nonstop snowboarding, it was almost as if I could hear the exuberant shouts of everyone else already up there, dropping cliffs, catching air, and getting perfect rides all up and down the mountain. I prided myself on being the first one up the lift in the morning and the last one off the slopes before nightfall. Now I'd be forced to stand in line, take my turn, and, worst of all, ride through snow that someone else had gotten to before me. I was anxious, obsessed in fact, with getting where I needed to be. I wasn't thinking about the necessities I should be taking with me. That was my first mistake.

Or maybe not. Maybe my first mistake was the attitude I brought along to the mountain in the first place. Back then, there was an arrogance I carried around with me like a chip on my shoulder, a selfish self-regard that always put me and my agenda first. After a year of consistent drug use—a carefully calibrated combination of crystal meth, potent marijuana, and alcohol—I had pretty much lost touch with the rest of the human race. I was a loner, the master of a world that I manipulated at will and shaped to my specifications. To say that I was a control freak doesn't begin to explain how I led my life in strict accordance with my own priorities. Whatever didn't meet my exacting standards, I simply discarded. And since people were far from predictable, they were the first to go.

It might have been different if there had been somebody else with me that day, a friend, a snowboarding buddy, someone to tell me to slow down and take it easy, that the mountain would still be there when I showed up. But I'd long since passed up the opportunity for companionship. I did what I did by myself and for myself and I liked it that way. I lived inside my own head, alone with my thoughts and my schemes and the satisfaction I got from pursuing perfection. A favorite coach of mine used to say, "Experience is something you won't get until after you need it." Since I didn't have it, I didn't know I needed it.

That day on the slope was going to be perfect, and I was already missing out. It was an intolerable situation. I moved quickly through the borrowed condo where I was staying, distracted by the sunlight filtering in through the high windows, haphazardly grabbing a few odds and ends without really thinking about what I was doing.

Why bother? I'd been up those slopes hundreds of times before. I knew Mammoth like the back of my hand. I'd spent as much time as I possibly could amid that stunning Sierra Nevada scenery, coming in from my home in Southern California dozens of times a season. I yearned to be up above the tree line at eleven thousand five hundred feet, where you could see the curvature of the earth. I had an intricate map of the snowboarding trails imprinted in my mind, the best tables, drops, and hits, the secret places where the cornices curled like frozen waves across the spine of the ridgebacks, the places few others ever went, where the powder was fresh and unmarked and waiting for me. I was totally familiar with this environment, completely acclimated and supremely self-confident in my ability to master the most difficult terrain. I owned that mountain. At least I thought I did.

Now that the storm had cleared, conditions were

optimal and I wasn't about to weigh myself down with a lot of unnecessary clothing and equipment. I had several different options that I'd brought with me in anticipation of the ever-changing weather conditions on the mountain, including a heavy-duty waterproof Gortex outfit. But I knew that would be bulky and unwieldy and that its thermal protection might be too much for such a pristine day. Instead I chose a Ripzone jacket and a pair of ski pants with zip-out linings that I immediately removed. I put on the stripped-down shell over my cotton boxer shorts and slipped on some regular gym socks and a long-sleeve T-shirt. I grabbed a thin beanie, spring gloves, and a small pair of goggles. My main concern was to stay as lightweight as possible. I was dressing for what the weather forecast said it would be: about twenty-seven degrees. I wasn't protected enough to keep me from getting cold as I rode up on the lifts, but I knew I would warm up on the rides, when my body was in motion.

I looked around for my boots, a pair of Burtons I had bought secondhand. When I first got them, I could still smell the stink from the previous owner's feet. The dude in the shop told me that they had been used by a pro rider. A pro rider was what I wanted to be. I'd sprayed them heavily with Lysol, which didn't help much, but I liked the boots primarily for their speed lacing system, which used a dial to cinch up the laces and made getting in and out of them much quicker and easier. As I said, I was in a hurry to get to the mountain that morning.

My snowboard was also a Burton, a 164.5-centimeter

"Code" model. A guy my size, 5'9.5", should have been using a smaller board, but I preferred the longer length for
its increased stability and strength for my big-mountain,
custom freestyle riding, which I took full advantage of. Its
shape was a little like a figure eight or a modified dog bone,
curving in at the middle and wider at the front and back. It
was made from laminated graphite, a tough, hard material
that was state of the art for snowboarding thanks to its
light weight and durability. The board was equipped with
ratchet bindings that could be adjusted for just the right
foot stance.

When I bought it, the board had been stamped as a
second because of some small flaw. It was cheaper than a
top grade model, which sealed the deal for me, but before
I took it, I asked, "Hey, brother, can you grind off the
marking?" I didn't want it known that I was riding anything other than the best. It was just another part of the
image I had constructed for myself, a mix of ego and drug
delusion. But in point of fact, I *was* one of the best, at least
when I was on my board. Coming down the slopes on a
great run, I could see others stopping just to watch me or
point me out to their friends, saying, "Dude, watch this
guy. He's awesome! He'll hit every jump." The way I saw it,
I had a reputation to uphold. Some of it, of course, was
drug-fueled ego, but there was also some truth to my high
self-regard. I had a natural flair for snowboarding.

Still imagining I could hear the amazed shouts of the
snowboarders on the slopes, I took a quick look around

the condo for whatever else I might need. I slipped a
twenty-dollar bill out of my wallet, thinking I'd use it for a
quick lunch at one of the lodges that dot the slope. Off the
kitchen counter, I scooped four pieces of Bazooka bubble
gum to chew while I was riding for a quick hit of sugar. I
grabbed my cell phone and my MP3 player, programmed
with the music I would use as a soundtrack for the day. I
had actually planned out which playlist I would select for
which run I would be on at any given time, matching my
moves to a particular song, which during that time included a lot of hip-hop and rap, especially Eminem.

The funny thing was, when I was actually out on the
slope and about to take a jump, I'd never hear the music I'd
so carefully sequenced. As I'd approach a ramp, building up
speed, I'd remind myself to listen to the song I'd prepared
for that very moment. But as soon as I got airborne, exhilaration would overtake me and my mind would empty. It
was one of the few times that would actually happen—
when the incessant chatter between my ears would fade to
nothing and I'd be part of the majestic emptiness around
me. Then, as soon as I returned to earth, the thudding beat
in my ears would return and I'd be back where I was before.

That morning I forgot to take a lot of things I normally
carry with me any time I ride. One of the most essential
was a two-way radio that had a range of about seven miles
and that I'd made a habit of carrying along no matter how
unencumbered I wanted to be. The same was true of a
torch lighter that I had originally bought to smoke my kush

in between runs. Because of the high altitude, most regular lighters didn't work, and I had made a point of finding one that could produce a flame even in the thinnest air. I would also normally pack a couple of apples with me, one to eat and the other to carve and punch out for a makeshift pipe, ducking down into the tree line for an occasional toke through the hollowed-out core. This time, instead of the fruit, I knocked back a couple of bottles of water and slipped one into my pocket to drink later. I was ready to go.

Except for one last item. Before I closed the door behind me, I patted the pocket of my jacket to make sure it was still there—a small plastic baggie with a half gram of high-quality crystal meth. That was one thing I made sure never to go anywhere without.

I HAD BEEN doing meth on a daily basis for the better part of a year, and by the time I arrived in Mammoth, on February 1, 2004, it was starting to catch up with me. I still harbored the illusion that I was in control of the drug and not the other way around, even though the gaunt face that greeted me in the mirror every morning said otherwise. My gums were receding, my skin had broken out, and I could see my haunted, hollow eyes staring back at me like a paranoid stranger's. There was no hiding what was happening to me: I was destroying my body. Yet, at the same time, I was focusing with all the obsession that the drug pumped into me on my physical condition. Being in good—make that

great—shape had been one of the most satisfying achievements in my life and one in which I took justifiable pride.
But it wasn't just the way I looked or was able to perform as
an athlete that made being ripped so significant. I genuinely
enjoyed working out, building muscle and endurance while
feeling the release of endorphins as I pushed past my own
limits and strived for a new and improved version of myself.
It was true that I had loved sports from the time I was a kid,
but what really gave me a sense of accomplishment was to
shape and hone my body, to make it responsive and resilient
and ready for any challenge. It was a big part of my identity
and made me feel more accomplished.

It wasn't the identity of the run-of-the-mill meth user.
For them, a wasted body was the price they paid for getting high, but I wasn't willing to pay that price. I continued to work out, intensely and methodically, even as I
continued to ingest the poison that was eating me away
from the inside.

I once heard a description of meth's effects that I'll
never forget: it is as if the wheels of a fine automobile, a
Maserati for example, have been mounted on rollers and
the car is revved to the max and left that way, running
twenty-four hours a day, until the engine burns out. It's going nowhere at a hundred miles an hour. So was I.

But I firmly believed that I *was* going somewhere, pushing myself to the limit and using the drug to fuel my crazed
pursuit of physical perfection. A good day for me would begin by snorting a couple of lines of speed, taking a couple of

hits on a bong, and heading over to the gym. Whenever I had the chance, I'd be snowboarding, surfing, or playing hockey. Two or three or five hours later, I'd head out to the beach, looking to surf or play some volleyball, then pedal home on my bicycle or back to the gym to soak in the Jacuzzi. All the focus and concentration that meth gave me, I put into building my body.

I was kidding myself. No matter how hard I exercised, no matter how intent I was on keeping myself in shape, there was just no way I could fully compensate for the degenerating effect of the drug. What had started out as a terrific side benefit—the way meth curbed my appetite and kept me lean and mean—soon turned into an alarming loss of weight and the inability to maintain the proper diet for my level of activity. I *was* getting gaunt, with dark circles under my eyes, the telltale signs of the downward addictive spiral.

Worse still, I was beginning to lose control of my motor skills and even the ability to translate thought and instinct into action. A few weeks before I'd headed up to Mammoth, I had cracked a beer late one night, getting ready to settle back and zone out on my second-favorite pastime, surfing the Internet. An hour later I looked up from the screen. The beer was just where I had left it, untouched. I'd forgotten all about it. Only then, when I finally reached for it, did I experience a strange disjunction between my mind and my muscles. My thoughts could send a signal to my body, but somewhere along the way, it was getting scrambled. It was like nothing so much as a string tied to my arm and holding me back. I'd become a puppet to my habit.

If I was frightened by what I was becoming, there was another part of me that just didn't care. I considered myself totally self-sufficient, as long as I had that little baggie of white powder with me at all times. My loner status was enhanced by the fact that I seemed to have completely forgotten how to relate to people. At bars or parties, I talked too loud, too fast, or too long until those around me would start to back off, a wary look in their eyes.

As time went on, my contact with the outside world diminished in rapid degrees. I didn't care about that either. I preferred being on my own, planning my workout regimens and attending to the thousand little details of my life that had to be perfectly executed. It got so that it was a real challenge just to leave the house. It would literally take hours of preparation before I could walk out the door. The shower had to be just the exact temperature I required, and every bottle of bath oil had to be lined up in its proper sequence. I would shave down every trace of stubble and comb my hair until it was perfectly in place. Trying to pick what outfit to wear was a major undertaking involving dozens of possible combinations, and more often than not, by the time I was finally ready to leave, I'd decide I'd rather stay home anyway, pecking away at the computer keyboard until the break of dawn. I tried to keep up my regimen at the gym and still spend time at the beach, but even these activities were done in isolation and had to be planned out in every detail.

There was only one thing that got me out of the narrowing confines of that self-imposed exile from reality. There is something so simple, so elemental about the joy of snowboarding that, in those few minutes during a run down fresh powder, I could forget all about myself and the crystal palace that had become my prison. Ask anyone who snowboards enough to get good at it. If words don't fail them completely, then they might try to explain that weightless, walking-on-water sensation that comes up through your feet and lifts your whole body. When it's freezing cold and the humidity is low and conditions are just right, you're pushed along as if by some invisible hand, cushioned by the snow that arcs up in a rainbow dusting whenever you make a turn. And sometimes the turns even make themselves, like when you're riding through the trees, kicking back and letting the board take you where it wants to go, following the contours of the mountain, weaving through the forest all by itself. When that happens, and you're just along for the ride, it's easy to give up control and just go with the flow. You're a part of the natural world and it's a part of you.

It might seem paradoxical. I was a slave to a drug that gave me a sense of total control. I was involved in a sport that removed the need for control. I was building up my body and tearing it down at the same time. I was an athlete and an addict. We're all creatures of contradiction, I guess, but my case was an extreme example. My whole life had been about testing my own limits. And I had some remarkable achievements to my credit. But there was still something missing. I was on a search, but I didn't even know what I was looking for.

CHAPTER TWO

The Apple

WHERE I WAS heading on that cold, clear February morning had a lot to do with where I'd come from. Through a wealth of experience, good, bad, and ugly, I've learned that nothing happens by accident. The circumstances that would shortly bring me to the brink of life and death had been guiding me steadily to this particular destination my whole life. I didn't realize it at the time, of course. I was too intent on getting where I wanted to be. It was only later that I could see clearly how I had come to the end of one long road, and to the beginning of another.

If I had to pick a point where I first encountered my destiny and realized that there was a purpose for my life, I'd have to tag it to a time when I was four years old, on a sunny Southern California day in the suburb of West Hills at the far west end of the San Fernando Valley. I remember it vividly. I was riding down the sidewalk on my Big Wheel, pumping those plastic pedals for all I was worth, when I suddenly came to a dead stop. The sight of two neighborhood kids playing transfixed me. Each of them was wielding a strange stick I'd never seen before, with a flat curved edge at the bottom. Between them they were knocking a thick black disc back and forth, trying to slide it past each other. In that one moment my life changed forever. Whatever it was that they were doing, I wanted to do, too. I had discovered hockey. Or maybe it had discovered me. Either way, it was destiny.

I had already lived a pretty eventful childhood, although, of course, I had nothing to compare it to. It seemed completely normal to me that a kid my age should already have lived on two continents, speak two languages, and have the kind of dual identity that came along with that experience. My father, Phillip, was a Frenchman who had met my mother, Susan, in New York. They fell in love, got married, and returned briefly to France, where I was born, in Paris, in July of 1969.

I've always considered myself completely and totally American. But my French identity would later come to play an important role in my life, both professionally and personally. It helped me to take a broader view of the world, to see things from different perspectives and to go for opportunities that I otherwise would have missed. I feel lucky to have that mixed heritage, and I've made the most of it.

My father was a chef by profession, a specialist in

pastries, and after we moved back to the United States when I was still an infant, he set about building a successful career for himself in the restaurant business. He settled his young family in Los Angeles and went on to open three very successful establishments, Papillon, Bourbon Street, and the Bicycle Shop Café, which he owned and operated for over thirty-five years. Some of my earliest memories were of crawling around under restaurant tables, terrorizing the customers.

But before we came to Southern California, we stayed for a short time with my mother's parents in Florida. It was there that I first encountered one of the most memorable and influential individuals in my life, my grandfather. A former Golden Gloves champion boxer, a lifeguard, and a varsity athlete in four sports, he had grown up on the mean streets of Hell's Kitchen in New York City. A parish priest there had originally taught my grandfather to fight, defending his thirteen brothers and sisters from neighborhood toughs, and it was that same hard-boiled, no-nonsense attitude that he passed on to me. My grandfather was tough, physically and mentally, a child of the Depression who was used to struggle and hardship. I vividly remember coming home crying when a neighborhood bully picked on me, and my grandfather's response to me: "Why come home and complain? Go punch him in the nose so he'll never bother you again." An hour later my grandfather heard a knock on the door. It was the bully's parents, complaining about my rough treatment of their son. "Good," he promptly replied. "It's about time someone knocked him around a little."

We have a saying in hockey: "It's not how many fights you win or lose that makes you tough. It's how many fights you're in that makes you tough." That could have been his motto. Nothing had come easy for him, and his steely determination was his greatest gift to me. It was a determination that I would call up time and again in the ordeal I was about to undergo on Mammoth Mountain. In many ways, I credit the spirit of my grandfather, and the rugged individuality that he had cultivated in me, with saving my life.

The first opportunity I had to display that spirit was shortly after I had stood spellbound watching those kids playing street hockey. Within a few days I had begged, pleaded, and cajoled my parents into buying me some equipment and signing me up on a local kids' team. At that time, of course, the idea of playing hockey in the Golden State was hard for a lot of people to get their heads around. Naturally, the sport had trouble putting down roots in a place known for its endless summer, and hockey players, not to mention the infrastructure to support them, were scarce. It was not until the great Wayne Gretzky came to the Los Angeles Kings in 1988 that the game would become really popular in the state. The popularity of Rollerblades helped, simulating the speed and action of skating on a frozen pond.

I was living in the land of surf and sun, and in fact, I enjoyed hanging out at the beach, surfing, and skateboarding around the neighborhood as much as the next California kid. But it was on one of the few ice rinks in the area, in a mall off Topanga Canyon Boulevard not far from our home, that I really came into my own. If you'd asked me back then what I wanted to be when I grew up, I could have answered without hesitation: a hockey player. Even though I was short and kind of chubby, nothing held me back. I spent as much time on that rink as I could, showing up in the early morning, which was the only time the team could practice, before the place opened up for its regular ice skating business.

Actually, most of the time I didn't wait for the morning. I'd go to bed, half dressed in my hockey uniform, sleeping between my hockey sheets featuring famous team logos, ready for action as soon as my mother came in to drive me to the rink. From the beginning, she and my father were totally supportive of my enthusiasm for hockey. It was a support that would translate into countless hours and substantial sums of money as I pursued my ambition. Even back then, I was aiming high: selecting for my jersey the famed number 4 of Bobby Orr. My colors, of course, were those of the legendary American hockey dynasty, the Boston Bruins, coincidently a club I would later play for.

I was eight years old when my parents divorced. For the next several years, I bounced back and forth between their homes, and when I lived with my father, I got a real taste of the Hollywood high life. His restaurant was the hub of the fast-lane scene in LA at that time, and it was there that I had my first real exposure to sex, drugs, and rock 'n' roll.

My dad, who had a very old-school European macho attitude, was not exactly the best role model for a growing boy. At age twelve, he was letting me drive his car, and I had my first taste of marijuana and cocaine in the back room of his establishment. There were lots of willing young waitresses, and the manager of the place was a woman in her thirties who seduced me when I was fifteen. When I told my father I had had sex with her, he just laughed. "Good," he said. "That's what women are for." I later found out that he had slept with her, too. It was kind of creepy, but more than anything else, the experience taught me that it was acceptable to take what you want from others, that people were there to be used.

It was a different story at my mother's house. She had gone on to marry Jack White, a professional cartoon animator who hailed from Windsor, Ontario, and who happened to be my hockey coach. Like my grandfather, my stepdad was a great influence on my life, a natural motivator who I think coined the term "Just do it" long before it became an advertising slogan. He would accept no excuses and could care less about your blisters or sore ankles. "Just do it!" he'd shout. And I did. He taught me the essential equation for success in the game: a blend of physical and mental preparation combined with a passion for all the sport had to offer—the speed, the excitement, and most of all, the pure joy of it.

I started out as a goalie, which was the ideal position for understanding the game, how plays developed and the overall strategy of a winning team. "Your best offense is the best defense" was my stepfather's mantra. After that I became a forward left wing. Although I had a wicked right shot, my skill level allowed me to play the offside, being a right shooter but playing on the left side. I was able to pick up passes and make clean backhand passes with a quick release and had the ability to shoot one-timers, shooting the puck on the fly. I developed the adaptability that is all too often missing with a lot of players who learn to do one thing and one thing only. I could play offense, defense, and on both my strong and weak sides of the ice, and I still had my chops as a goalie, dressing and shutting down the opposing team. I was a total player—born for hockey.

But mostly I learned how to handle myself on the ice. My stepfather had the foresight to look beyond the gawky, overweight kid I was to see my potential as a power skater. I was quickly developing strength, speed, and control, and it got to the point where I could launch myself onto the ice from a standstill on one skate and glide, edging from the inside to the outside of my skate blade, around the rink three or four times without ever putting down my other foot. I was able to create my own momentum and reverse it on a dime, moving forward on a single skate blade, stopping and starting going forwards to backwards on the same blade. Spurred on by Jack, I worked hard to perfect my technique, working the edge of the skate, rolling up and off of it. I learned to generate power on an eight-inch-long, one-eighth-inch-wide laser-cut steel blade, using my skating ability to change gears while making turns and still moving forward. I was getting good. Very good.

AND, AS UNLIKELY as it seemed that a California team could make its mark in hockey, we began racking up a solid string of victories. First we moved up the ranks of the few other junior teams in the state, and then went regional. I was singled out to play tournaments on the California All-Star team at age ten and made the cut every year. By that time I had already established a reputation as a youngster to watch, catching the attention of NHL's Central Scouting program. My standing was enhanced when, in the ninth grade, our team made it to the Nationals, an unheard-of accomplishment for a team from California. The team I played with was part of the so-called Bantam League, the AAA Traveling Hockey organization for fourteen- and fifteen-year-olds. We were beaten that year by a team from Detroit, but it was a measure of my abilities on the rink that, as soon as the game was over, the Detroit team, which was sponsored by Compuware, approached me to play for them. Their coach was Real Turcotte, the sire of the famed hockey family that included Alfie Turcotte, who was playing for the Montreal Canadiens at the time.

It was a great opportunity. Michigan, of course, was right in the heart of hockey country "Hockeytown USA," but in order to accept the offer, I'd have to move there. That was a no-brainer. With my parents' consent and encouragement, I relocated to Milford, Michigan, in the southeastern part of the state, to finish high school. After seeing me play, Coach Turcotte not only offered me a spot on the team, but also agreed to put me up in his home for the duration.

It was like I'd died and gone to heaven. Of course, I missed my parents. I even missed the glimpses of the California sunshine I used to see going to and from practice sessions at my old rinks. But my homesickness was more than offset by being in a place where hockey was the number one priority and hockey players were the local superstars. I'd always been a good student, but suddenly it didn't much matter anymore. School was no big deal. It was all about how you handled yourself, and the team I was on was one of the best. During our first season, we won a hundred games and lost three. We were, simply put, the hottest thing on and off the ice. Winning the Nationals came easily and I was voted Most Valuable Player—a natural-born superstar in the making.

It seemed to me I had good reason to think so. In 1986 my stepdad was hired as a consultant for a hockey film called *Youngblood* that starred Rob Lowe and Patrick Swayze, who was just beginning to make a name for himself in Hollywood. I was asked to help Swayze become familiar with some of the basic moves of the game, and we ended up spending a lot of time together. It was clear to me that I had taken the first giant step toward securing my own fame and fortune. I was hanging out with movie stars. But hockey came first. By the time I graduated high school, I had already been recruited by a couple of Junior A semi-pro teams, which essentially served as farm clubs for the National Hockey League. It was a tempting offer. There was no school involved, you were paid to play and allowed to fight. Of course, I'd already been involved in more than a few scraps on and off the ice. My grandfather had taught me how to stick up for myself, and I'd get a lot of experience doing just that in the junior league.

But in the end, I turned down offers from both Seattle and Saskatoon. The fact that my parents were concerned that I should have an education to fall back on after my hockey career had a lot to do with my decision. So, too, did the counsel of Walt Kyle, who is now the head coach of Northern Michigan University and yet another key influence in my life. Kyle, an NHL coach who twice battled cancer successfully, was a coach's coach, tough and demanding but also supremely motivating and inspirational. He was a big part of the reason why I decided to pick college.

At seventeen I moved up to Marquette, Michigan, which is about as far north as you can get in the state before stepping over into Canada, becoming the third youngest player to play NCAA Division 1 college hockey. We used to joke that we looked forward to storms because the blanket of snow would warm it up to twenty degrees. I spent the next four years there, at Northern Michigan University, training harder than I ever had in my life, working up to regular twenty-mile runs before every season and topping them off with a plunge into ice-cold Lake Superior. We'd practice nearly every day and play every weekend and somehow find time in between to attend classes. Although getting a degree wasn't my highest priority, I stuck to my studies as best as I could, majoring in marketing because I thought it might come in handy down the road. I later wanted to change my major but was advised against it. I might as well have something to show for my college years, since it was all but certain that I was going on to play pro. It didn't really matter what educational route I took as long as I got a degree.

In fact, there was never really any doubt which road I was heading down. My time in college was focused on one thing: moving me toward a professional hockey team. Even though I knew that the average career in the NHL was less than three years, I had hopes of a longer run. I was young, strong, and had well-developed skills. It would have been impossible to persuade me that there wasn't a promising future in the Apple waiting for me. But at that point, it wasn't entirely about me. I wanted to take care of my parents, as well. They had sacrificed so much to get me to the brink of the big time. I wanted to be able to give something back, to make good on their investment of time and money.

Looking back, I can see how it was all too rushed: too much, too soon, with too little time to prepare. The fact was, my own expectations had run far ahead of my maturity. With the exception of my physical abilities, in most ways I was still a kid. I had been driving myself relentlessly for most of my life, pushing toward a single goal and neglecting the process of growing up and getting to know what life, in all its diversity, was about. Here I was, barely out of my teens, and already thrusting myself as fast and as hard as I could into a highly competitive adult world, with all the responsibilities, temptations, and emotional demands that came with it. I just didn't have the emotional maturity.

Not that it mattered. My course had already been charted. At age seventeen, immediately after I had been enrolled at NMU, I had been drafted into the NHL. The Bruins chose me in the ninth round out of an overall field of more than two hundred, and it was like some childhood fantasy coming true. I had slept in Bruin colors as a kid, dreaming of glory with the fabled Boston team, and now it had all come true.

They say to be careful what you wish for, but as far as I was concerned I had wished for the best and that's exactly what I'd gotten. For four years while I attended college, the franchise kept an eye on me, watching me develop and biding their time until I was old enough to make my debut in what they called the Apple, hockey terminology for the big leagues. Thanks to a generous signing bonus, they owned the rights to make that call whenever they saw fit. But as it turned out, it wasn't soon enough for me.

The first move the Bruins made after I graduated was to show me off in a couple of exhibition games. It was a thrill unlike any other I'd experienced to take the ice with a team that had meant so much to me. I performed well and expected to be given a slot in the lineup. But instead, I was told I would be sent to the club's AAA team, the Maine Mariners, for further development. That wasn't what I wanted to hear.

In retrospect, I wasn't the best fit for the team in the first place. The Bruins were renowned for their big players, and although I was tough and scrappy, I was also 5'9.5" and 185 pounds. I didn't fit their mold, but you couldn't tell me that. I thought I had earned my spot and then some. Whatever I lacked in size, I made up for in ego, and it hurt my pride to be sent to the minors, even though the Mariners were an excellent team. In hockey parlance, league teams were called the Cranapple, as opposed to the major league Apple. I knew which one I wanted a bite out of.

It was obviously a disappointment not to play for the Bruins in the regular season, but by that time I had gotten another offer, one that sounded pretty good to me. A representative for a French team approached me with an offer to play. While the rules were pretty strict about recruiting players who were not nationals, I was able to qualify because of my dual citizenship. As much as to express

my frustration with the Bruins as to have a definite plan
for my career, I decided to take the job.

It seemed ideal. I was paid seventy-five thousand
dollars after taxes, played a shortened season, and was provided with a BMW and a furnished apartment at the base of
the French Alps. But as I would come to find out, there was
an upside and a downside to the decision I had made. On
the one hand, I had the opportunity to play some of the
best, and most exciting, hockey of my life. In Europe, where
the game is played on a bigger rink, the action is generally
faster, stretched out and wide open, with more skating and
scoring opportunities involved. There is no red line that put
a limit on who you could pass to and a lot less clutching and
grabbing. All of these rules have now been incorporated
into the NHL, thanks to the influx of European players. As
part of a French team, I had an opportunity to play some
of the fiercest competitors in the world—the Swedes,
Russians, Finns, and Czechs, teams with hockey traditions
that went far back into sports history.

On the other hand, as an American, Europe was a
place you went to finish out your career, not get it started.
But don't get me wrong—I enjoyed playing there, and the
money was good.

And compared to the schedule I had to maintain with
Coach Kyle, my new training and playing calendar left me
a lot of time for skiing those mountains looming over my
apartment. But I still had ambitions of hoisting the
Stanley Cup, and no matter how good the hockey might

have been, that wasn't going to happen from three thousand miles away.

I had a chance to return to the States in 1992 to play for the Los Angeles Kings' farm team in San Diego. But the situation there made it even less likely that I'd get out of the Cranapple and into the Apple. There just weren't that many slots available in the Kings organization. They had just lost to the Montreal Canadiens in the Stanley Cup finals that season. Only later did I realize the importance of an agent in finding a good match between a player and a team. Instead of trying to find a slot with the two strongest teams of the time, I would have had a better chance to move up by joining an expansion team.

I returned to France, determined to make the best of the situation I found myself in. For the next three years I played exclusively for France, and it was during that time that I reached my peak as a player. Looking back, I take a lot of pride in the commitment and energy I gave to the game at that time. Hockey can be a very humbling sport. One minute you can be a plus-four player, skating on top of the world. The next, you'll cough up the puck and watch helplessly as it slides into your own net. It can make you a hero or a goat, in the course of the same game.

I never really realized how difficult hockey was until I tried other sports, like beach volleyball, or even golf. As demanding as they might be, none compared to tearing around the ice at thirty miles an hour, making decisions on a split-second basis and thinking three steps ahead to

make the play. You have to have incredible coordination
and the ability to take a hit and bounce right back. An old
locker room saying goes, "There's being in shape and then
there's being in hockey shape." For a long time I kept myself in hockey shape.

The highlight of my time playing for France has to be
when I was recruited for the National team to play in the
1994 Winter Olympics in Lillehammer, Norway. It was an
incredible honor just to have been asked to participate in
the games, especially as a member of one of the top three
teams in the European League. We played against the
Americans in a tie game that had a lot of people talking at
the time: what was an American doing on the French
team, especially one that could skate the U.S. to a draw,
scoring three of the four goals?

But by that time, the handwriting was already on the
wall regarding my future in the sport. After the Olympics,
I joined a German team where I played for two years, off
and on from 1996 to 1998, but by then I was beginning to
have some serious physical problems. I'd taken my share
of abuse on the ice, of course: broken teeth and fingers, a
dislocated shoulder, and over sixty stitches in my face
alone. At one point I had sustained major nerve damage
when a puck rebounded off my eye socket. A wild stick
tore a hole in my nose so big I could breathe through it.

But that kind of pain you learn to live through. When
bulging discs in my back started giving me trouble, it was a
different story. It was getting to the point that I was hav-

ing trouble bending over and tying my shoes. I knew that if I stopped playing, I'd have a chance to heal, and the truth was, I had more or less come to the end of the line as a player. My NHL dreams of signing a big contract had long since faded, and as much as I appreciated being able to compete with and against some of the best players in the world, the thrill of the game had begun to fade for me. I was thirty years old and I had the rest of my life to live. It was time to make my next move.

Coaching was the obvious choice. I knew the game inside out, had the ability to pick out and nurture talent, and I was good with kids, learning how to relate to them when I took a summer job coaching at the Turcottes' hockey camp. It was there that I was able to pass along many of the motivational techniques I had learned from my grandfather, Coach Kyle, and others. I was also able to utilize my coaching skills in the Cranapple when I returned to the States and briefly played and assisted in coaching in Little Rock, Arkansas.

It didn't last long. I quickly discovered that I had gotten accustomed to a more active life, and, while Little Rock was a pleasant enough place, I found myself craving a little more freedom and variety than what I was getting coaching five days a week for a salary that just barely covered my expenses.

About that time I got a call from Easton Sports, one of the top manufacturers of athletic equipment in the world. Known especially for their high-quality aluminum baseball bats, bicycles, arrows, and camping gear, the company was looking for someone with a sports background to head up a grassroots marketing effort in the hockey department, with the emphasis on expanding their hockey business. I was intrigued by the opportunity for travel and the chance to expand my contacts in sports circles. I took the job without a second thought.

I relocated to Los Angeles and moved in with my mother. In many ways it was like picking up where I'd left off when I'd first gone to Michigan to chase my hockey dreams. Here I was back at home, getting my laundry done and my meals cooked. But I really didn't have much of a chance to enjoy my delayed adolescence. Easton kept me constantly on the road, visiting tournaments, athletic events, and sporting goods stores from coast to coast. And when I wasn't out promoting the Easton brand, I lent a hand in product development, helping to create advanced "twigs"—hockey slang for sticks, which had evolved from wood to aluminum to a composite—as well as coming up with new advances in their protective line and in skate design.

It was in 1999, while I was on the road for Easton, that I made a customer call in Beaver Creek, Colorado, near the famed Vail ski resort, and happened to see some kids out on the slope snowboarding. It was a moment not unlike that one twenty-five years earlier on the sidewalk of my neighborhood. It looked like fun. I decided to become a snowboarder.

CHAPTER THREE

Tweaking

IN LATE JANUARY of 2004, barely a week before I came up to Mammoth Mountain to catch one of the biggest winter storms of the season, the downward spiral of my life suddenly took a steep turn for the worse.

I had spent the day as usual, consumed by a hundred and one chores that added up to nothing. When I first started using meth, I discovered that I had a previously undiscovered talent for fixing things. Prior to that, I'd never been mechanically inclined, and now suddenly I discovered the ability to take apart the most complicated mechanical or electronic device, figure out how it worked, and put it back together again. More than anything, I think it was a symptom of how the perimeters of my existence were shrinking down to a vanishing point. My focus was getting smaller and smaller, my attention drawn into the tiniest of details.

When I wasn't tinkering away my time, I'd be putting

together elaborate camping trips, mostly at beach sites where I could set myself up with all the comforts of home. I'd spend most nights out surfing in the dark with a glow stick tied to my wetsuit. When there was no surf, I would write out my delusional thoughts in the wet sand, scanning the water for shark fins.

It's a process anyone addicted to speed for any length of time is all too familiar with. The world becomes a million moving parts and you're the master craftsman who manipulates it all. That is, until your own gears start slipping.

At that point there was nothing left to pull me out of the plummeting nosedive I was in. In the aftermath of 9/11, I had quit my job at Easton Sports, telling myself I was too nervous to fly as much as my schedule required. I think the truth was I just didn't want to work anymore. It had been a rough transition for me, going from my soaring ambitions as a hockey player to a working stiff with a paycheck that never seemed quite adequate. After three years I'd had enough, and used the terrorist attacks as an excuse to walk away, cashing in my 401(k) and drifting aimlessly as long as the money lasted. It was then that I began to seriously descend into drug abuse.

Even though I was quite comfortable living off my mother's largesse, picking up my teenage years where I had left off, I was also a little bit ashamed of myself. Here I was, thirty and still hanging out at home. Those were the kind of people I used to laugh at: the losers and deadbeats who couldn't get it together. Now I was one of them.

In order to assuage my guilt, I had briefly moved into a big sprawling place in the Tarzana hills with a buddy of mine who had a heavy meth habit and a posse of twenty-four-hour party people. It was here that I first really began using drugs on a regular basis, and it quickly became my primary reason for getting up in the morning. The place became a virtual drugstore and I was in the middle of it. When I wasn't hanging out with the sketchy characters at the house, I was wasting my time with one of the three dealers I had lined up to make sure I had a steady supply of crystal. Usually I'd bring over a couple of six-packs of beer that would gain admission to the day's activities: getting high while a stream of customers came and went. One of my connections lived in a dank hole at the far end of the valley, sharing the house with a woman who had two small children. They would crawl around on the filthy floor in dirty diapers, crying for attention while their mother traded sex for drugs in a bathroom. Even with my conscience numbed by meth, the plight of those kids bothered me. But I didn't dare say anything for fear of offending the drug supplier. I've always considered my silence an act of moral cowardice, but at the time the difference between right and wrong could be measured by a line of speed on a mirror.

The horror and shame of my condition didn't even

penetrate when, after falling asleep at that dealer's house one night, I woke up to find the floor crawling with cockroaches. I would soon enough be crawling myself, when there was a shortage in the meth supply and I got on my hands and knees to search through the carpet for any discarded speck of the drug.

As my meth use spiraled out of control, so, too, did the insanity and paranoia that plagued my mind. I once actually called the cops because I was sure there were intruders trying to break through the roof. It turned out to be scampering squirrels. The cops advised me to get some rest. At another low point, my obsessional behavior manifested itself by uncontrollable picking and tearing at my skin. I would often have to change shirts after the self-inflicted wounds bled through and stained whatever I was wearing.

I was hardly in a condition to take responsibility for myself, and eventually ended up back where I'd started, at my mom's house. By that time I was pretty much tapped out and I started teaching private hockey lessons to make ends meet. I found that I could get as much work as I wanted, mostly through word of mouth, but I was careful not to take on too many students. I wanted to reserve as much time as possible for my overriding obsession. I was living for me and only for me. Since that day in Beaver Creek, I had devoted myself totally to snowboarding. While I was still at Easton Sports, I'd take an extra couple of days from a business trip whenever I could to hit the slopes. I always made sure I got my work done, but the company was essentially paying for my off time. During my last years with them, I managed to rack up over two hundred days snowboarding, and as a result, I had reached a peak of performance on the slopes.

I even considered going professional, especially after watching the X Games, which was the first big event to promote the sport. I realized I was every bit as good as the guys who were making good money at riding. I could hit the big air, do the three-sixties and one-eighties and make every jump I went after without even thinking about it.

But, even given my skill level and the amount of time I dedicated to snowboarding, there was no way I was going to make it into the pro ranks. My drug use was undermining any resolve I might have had to get out of the rut I was in, and my circuits were too scrambled to sort out the steps I'd have to take.

By the beginning of 2004, it was all starting to come apart. One night, after a long session of tweaking and a late visit to the gym, the relentless pace I'd been keeping suddenly caught up with me. I pulled off to the side of the road and took out my bag of meth. I needed a pick-me-up to get me through the rest of my constant, aimless activities.

But somewhere along the way, I lost track of what I was doing, and the next thing I knew, I was wakened out of a sudden sleep by a knocking on my car window. It was the police. Apparently I'd pulled off the road in the hills of

Studio City right onto someone's property and fallen asleep, the bag of speed still sitting in my lap. I was arrested for trespassing and drug possession.

I spent the next five days in jail, the first time I'd ever been incarcerated in my life. My mother was doing her best to arrange my bail, but she was having a hard time dealing with the reality of who her son had become. Prior to my arrest, I had been careful to hide my drug use from her, staying away from the house when I was really high and making sure none of my meth buddies ever came around to visit. The truth was, my mother really had no idea what I was up to and it was a real shock when she got a phone call from me in lockup. Under the circumstances, I wouldn't have blamed her if she had just let me sit in there until my system had a chance to cleanse itself and I had the opportunity to take a good hard look at what was happening to me.

No chance. The wake-up call I needed wasn't going to happen behind bars. Even a gangbanger in lockup could see that I was heading for trouble. "Hey, brother," he warned me as I was being processed out, "take it slow out there, you hear me?" Good advice, but instead I went to the impound lot to get my ride and drove back to my dealer for a few lines of speed.

Up until the point of my arrest, I'd been tracking a major winter weather front that was rolling down across the Sierra Nevada range from Alaska. I had become something of an amateur meteorologist, checking online reports and the Weather Channel on a regular basis to stay on top of the best possible conditions for riding. This storm looked like it was going to leave behind some epic conditions, and here I was, stuck in jail. My main concern was to get out and get up to the mountain while the powder was still fresh.

When I was finally released, I was given a court date to appear for a hearing three weeks later, on a Tuesday. That would give me the better part of ten days to be out on the slopes, and I didn't waste any time. Of course, I still had my schedule of private hockey lessons to teach, but, as I had done many times before, I hastily rearranged my calendar to make room for the trip.

Even at this point in my drug addiction, I still got a lot of satisfaction out of teaching. It felt good to be able to encourage and motivate kids, to develop their latent talents and pass along the techniques and skills I had developed over the years. In a way, they were like a family to me, and I took my responsibilities toward them very seriously. I had obviously compromised that responsibility when I got arrested, but was able to excuse my absence with a few convenient lies.

I had more excuses to explain my absence when I left for the mountain. When there was a possibility of powder, that became my number one priority and I didn't think twice about blowing off my students to get to the snow. It was selfish, for sure, but when I look back on it, I can see another reason for the sense of urgency I felt.

Snowboarding was a way for me to get away from the tension and strife in my life, especially those that resulted from my drug use. As a rule, I wouldn't use meth when I was riding. I didn't want to spoil the peace and happiness and sense of contentment that came from being so close to nature and from letting go of the guilt and feelings of failure that plagued me. After my stint in jail, my body was beginning to cleanse itself, but as soon as I got out I went straight to my dealer to replenish my stash, and by the time I made it to the mountain I had plenty of meth coursing through my system.

Even though I couldn't escape from myself, snowboarding offered me a momentary respite from the incessant voices in my head. I would bring the drugs with me, of course. It was like a security blanket that I couldn't do without. But when I was really in my element, riding from first light of morning until the final fade of twilight, meth was the last thing I needed. I had found the tranquility that proved so elusive in the rest of my life.

THE PARENTS OF one of my students had a condo at Mammoth, and I had previously arranged to exchange some lessons for a few days' use of the place. The next thing I needed was a ride. After getting out of jail, I had gone on a meth run for a few days. I knew I needed to get some rest if I wanted to be at my best on the slopes. For that reason I wanted to avoid having to drive up myself and, instead, caught a ride with a lady friend of a next-door neighbor, a woman I barely knew, who was taking a trip up north with her family. I'd have to find a way to get back in time for my hearing on Tuesday, but I wasn't worrying about that. Something would come up.

My main objective was to get up there just before the storm hit to maximize my chances of optimal conditions. I had made arrangements with my ride to pick me up at five in the afternoon, but she didn't show up until after eight in the evening, and by that time, I was antsy and irritated. It was February 1, Superbowl Sunday, and while I was packing, I watched the game, between the New England Patriots and the Carolina Panthers, out of the corner of my eye. I must not have been paying much attention, because I totally missed Janet Jackson's infamous "wardrobe malfunction" during the halftime show. The fact was, I had my mind on one thing and one thing only. It was the mountain that loomed before me, obscuring everything else.

I slept most of the way up, or tried to anyway. I still had meth in my system and was pretty keyed up about finally reaching my destination. But as we got closer to the mountain, the car had trouble negotiating the icy roads and I had to get out in the middle of the freezing night to put on chains. That didn't help to improve my mood, either. I insisted on driving the rest of the way and was quickly pulled over for speeding.

I was able to sweet-talk my way out of a ticket and the

fact that I didn't even have my license with me. I could be very charming and convincing when the situation demanded, and the cop let me go with a warning.

We got in late and I was dropped off at the borrowed condo. I had the key, of course, but the lock mechanism at the front door had frozen and I couldn't get it to open. Half out of necessity and half out of frustration, I kicked it ajar and in the process badly bruised my foot. I went straight to bed, tired enough now to fall into a deep sleep, but when I woke up the next morning, my foot was throbbing painfully and I had a worrisome limp.

But that wasn't going to stop me. Nothing was going to stop me. I was out early the next day. It took me a little longer to get to the gondola that carried riders to the slopes inside the park, because I didn't have a car and had to wait for the shuttle bus.

When I finally got up to the runs, I found myself in the middle of a storm that was dumping heavy loads of snow and reducing visibility to just a few feet. It was hardly the best conditions, but I didn't care. I was where I wanted to be and part of the experience was to adjust myself to whatever challenge the mountain threw up from moment to moment. I was hard core, or so I thought.

Because the air was colder above the ground than on the surface, a thick fog developed that clung to the slopes and forced me to ride slowly and cautiously. It took a lot of skill to negotiate that environment, but that was also part of what made it so enjoyable. That and the fact that there was no one out there to spoil the virgin runs.

The art of snowboarding had become second nature for me. I had spent time perfecting the techniques that would maximize speed and maneuverability, getting comfortable on both edges of the board and honing my ability to ride switch—with either the left or the right foot forward. I could link my turns to pick up speed without slowing down and feel the entire turn from the front edge through the tail end of the board, pop-springing out each turn and catching air. I could pull off most of the dazzling tricks that the pro riders did—dropping a cliff or doing a tumble roll—but that wasn't the point. I had nothing to prove. I was out there for the pure joy of it, using the tables and rails and jumps that dotted the slopes as my own personal playground.

Of course, that playground was limited by the severity of the storm. A lot of the more difficult runs had been closed by the ski patrol because of the blizzard, especially those rated Double Black Diamond. Ski and snowboarding trails are classified according to degree of difficulty, starting with a Green Circle, indicating wide and well-groomed slopes with a gradual gradient. Double Black Diamond specifies the most difficult rides, reserved for the most expert riders. The trails are steep and narrow. There is generally a lot of exposure to wind and steep drop-offs that require the highest level of skill to avoid dangerous or even lethal wipeouts. Most of the runs within the confines of the Mammoth Mountain ski park are in the beginner to intermediate—Blue Square—range, while many of the best Double Black Diamond slopes are at the very edges of its perimeter. Those were definitely off-limits during the storm.

For the next four days, I rode virtually from sunup to sundown, gradually moving to the more difficult slopes as the storm lessened and the mountain was progressively opened up. I'd plan my runs the night before, choosing slopes based on what direction they were situated and favoring north-facing descents because they were generally colder, which made the powder conditions last longer.

After a full day, I'd go to the nearby Juniper Springs Resort to use its spa, then meander back to the condo to get dressed for the evening. After getting high, I'd head over to the local bars where I knew I could fill up on happy hour appetizers. Then I'd head back to the condo to watch TV until I fell asleep. After eight hours of snowboarding, I'd left it all on the mountain, as we say in the sport, and it felt good.

When Friday morning dawned, my fifth day on the mountain was bright and clear, with visibility that seemed to extend to the far horizon and beyond. As I hurried to get myself together and make up for the time I'd lost by oversleeping, I made a decision to forgo my morning exercise and stretching. I usually prepared myself for riding with a half-hour stretch, loosening my muscles and getting in tune with my body. It was a way to wake up and get ready for the day, but there was no time to spare that morning. Overeager and underequipped, I rushed out of the condo and headed toward the shuttle stop.

As I rushed through the cold morning, I knew I'd be in for more frustration if I had to wait in line for the bus. I decided to hitchhike instead. It was the first time I'd ever done that, and looking back, I can see that the drugs, along with the rootless lifestyle I had slipped into, were clouding my judgment on matters large and small. I never thought of myself as the kind of guy who would be standing at the side of the road with his thumb out, depending on strangers to get me where I needed to go. But there I was, and it didn't seem to matter.

After a few minutes I was picked up.

"Where are you heading?" the driver asked.

"Heaven," I said. "Just get me to the nearest lift."

Instead, he dropped me off in the middle of town and I still had a hike to get to the gondola. It took me up the mountain to where the lifts branched off to various runs, and I took the first available ride to the top. The view from around twelve thousand feet was spectacular, the high peaks of the Sierra Nevada spread out in every direction and the sun glancing off the fresh, thick fall of snow. I made several runs, working my way west toward a spot called Back Door, a steep and demanding section that I hoped would still be relatively unoccupied.

I was right. I had the place pretty much to myself, and

over the next few hours I rode down untracked powder, coming slowly back to the east toward the more populated section of the park, where I planned to end the day. Some compartment in the back of my mind was aware of the fact that I wasn't really equipped for staying out too much longer. By 3:30 p.m. the sun was beginning to dip behind the mountain and the snow was showing the first signs of getting icy. I stood at the base of the slope near a lift, considering my options.

At that point I turned and looked east. What I saw was a huge bank of dark looming clouds rolling toward me from about two miles away. The storm that had hung over the resort for five days was coming back. It was moving with startling speed, consuming everything in its path in a thick, heavy fog. I watched for a minute and then headed for the lift. If I hurried, I could still get that last ride.

CHAPTER FOUR

Beyond the Edge

WITH THE STORM fast approaching, I rode down to the base station at the western end of the park. I hustled over to the gondola that would take me up the slopes for my final run before the blizzard swallowed up the terrain. As far as I was concerned, the unexpected change in weather was good news. The new snow would cover all the tracks of other riders along the trails, and there would be fresh conditions to enjoy in the morning.

The gondola took me to the top of the mountain and I rode over to the eastern ridge. As soon as I got off, it stopped, the hum of the cables fading away in the vastness. That seemed a little strange to me. Why were they shutting down the lifts? But it didn't change my mind about getting in one last run. I only found out later that the ski patrol had halted all activity and were escorting people off the mountain in anticipation of the storm's return. My plan was to hit a huge jump called the pipeline cornice, a lip of frozen snow that forms along the edge of a ridge like a solid wave and creates a perfect launch pad for an epic jump. You can soar as much as twenty or thirty feet if you get going fast enough and hit the cornice at just the right angle, surfing it before launching yourself into bliss.

I lined myself up perfectly and hit big air just as I'd hoped. It was the end of another perfect day of riding. I had now arrived at a little-used slope at the eastern extreme of the mountain called Beyond the Edge, at the tail end of Dragon's Back, a Double Black Diamond run with a lot of tricky turns that careened down along a narrow path. I had never been on the run before, which started about eleven thousand feet and headed down into a thick stand of trees. But I didn't hesitate. It seemed as if it would be a simple matter to take a shortcut down the slope from there, bearing east until I got back to the base station at Juniper Springs, and hit the gym, pool, and spa before heading back to the condo.

What I hadn't counted on was the speed and ferocity of the storm. Although I hadn't encountered any of the ski patrol crew that was, even then, busy clearing the slopes, I probably wouldn't have paid attention to them anyway. They would have been directing skiers and snowboarders to the various shuttle stops at the base of the mountain, and the last thing I wanted was to wait in line with everyone else for a seat on a bus back to town. I knew that if I could traverse the mountain at a west-to-east angle, I could make it down far enough to get back home on my own.

The Dragon's Back slope emptied into a wide, shallow bowl. The trick would be to get enough momentum to carry me through the half-mile-wide expanse and up to the ridge on the far side, where I'd be well situated at the top of another slope. Easy enough, but it was exactly at the moment when I started my descent that the storm caught up with me. Suddenly I was plunged into whiteout conditions with a howling wind in my face and a thick wall of fog blinding me. I knew that I was about to ride through a heavily forested area and that, if I wasn't careful, I could find myself wrapped around a trunk. I had no choice. Despite the fact that I needed to maintain my speed to be carried to the far side of the bowl, I had to slow down enough to avoid a collision.

Within a matter of seconds I had entered another dimension, one without length or breadth, a flat featureless landscape where the dark shapes of trees emerged from nowhere and whipped past me in the thick fog. I bobbed and weaved, doing my best to keep moving through the forest and up and over the smaller tree with ollies. But it wasn't enough. My velocity began to drop off. I was moving slower and slower and then, all at once, I was at a dead stop. *This is not good,* I told myself. The fun had come to a sudden halt.

I stood there for a moment, balanced on my board.

The wind whistled past my ears and I had to turn my face away from the snow flurries whipping around me. I tried to calmly evaluate my situation, but the reality of what had happened was only just beginning to register. At that point it was nothing more than an inconvenience. True, I was out in the middle of a major storm. No one knew where I was and I had only the most general idea of how to get back: going left would keep me in bounds; going right would take me deeper into the wilderness, out of bounds. But one thing was for sure. I wasn't going to be riding down to the safety and warmth of the condo unless I could somehow get out of that bowl.

I only had one option. I'd have to hike out. I wasn't happy about the prospect. In fact, I was thoroughly pissed off. Snowboarding is so effortless, so easy. It was the fastest and quickest way to get where I needed to go. Now, instead, I'd have to walk, slogging through the snow until I could get out of the shallow bottom I found myself in.

That would be easier said than done. When you're riding, your board essentially floats over the snow, your speed compensating for your weight and counteracting the effects of gravity. It's a whole different story when you're standing still on a small hunk of graphite. As soon as I stopped, the board sank with me on it until I was up to my knees in fine-grained powder. I reached down to unstrap myself and took a step forward. I immediately sank up to my thigh. Another fact became immediately clear: it was going to be hard, exhausting work to get myself out of there. The altitude also forces your lungs to work over-time.

For the next hour and a half, as the storm continued to dump a heavy mantle over the mountain and the shadows of the day grew longer, I pushed through the wilderness. Sometimes the snow was waist deep, sometimes higher. I was quickly panting for air from the high-altitude exertion and could feel the resiliency leeching out of my muscles as the residual meth in my system sapped my strength. Under the influence of the drug, there was no way to reserve my energy. My heart was pounding, my nerves were tense. I was on overdrive the entire time.

I started out by dragging my board behind me, but soon started using it as a scooting platform to make a trail for myself by packing down the snow in front of me. Whenever there was a slight slope on the valley floor, I'd kneel on my board and scoot myself down for as long as I could, even if it was only a few feet. Without really having the means to get my bearings, I knew I had to keep heading to the left, westerly, back into the groomed runs funneling down to the resort.

The storm showed no signs of abating and night was coming on quickly. Worse yet, I could feel my feet starting to get wet. The reason was simple. I was wearing entirely the wrong clothing for the circumstances I found myself in. The pants I had picked for their light weight, removing the heavier lining from the inside, had hooks that attached to my boots and a nylon sleeve that tucked up underneath to keep the snow out. The problem was, as I pushed my way through the deep snow, it packed up around my shins, soaking into my skin and running into my boots. My feet were soon drenched with ice-cold melt. It would have helped if I'd been wearing thicker, water-resistant ski socks, but all I had was a regular pair of gym socks that immediately became soggy.

The same was true of my hands and arms. After even a few minutes of literally digging myself forward inches at a time, my gloves and the sleeves of my thin jacket were also soaked. The heat of my body was melting the snow, but it was hard to tell whether it was that or the sweat that I was working up that was saturating me the most.

It was just about dark when I stumbled and clawed my way toward an eerily familiar patch of ground. It was then that I realized, with a stomach-churning jolt, that I had walked in a circle. In the fading light, I could see my own tracks heading off uphill into the fog, marking the exhausting progress I had made back to where I started. The angle of the bowl and the encroaching night, not to mention my own impatience, had played tricks with my sense of direction. By constantly bearing left, I had actually doubled back on myself.

At that moment, my emotions simplified themselves considerably. My irritation and impatience were gone. I wasn't afraid. Not yet. Instead, I felt a surge of determination, which, in its own way, was also familiar. It was as if all the life lessons I had learned from my grandfather, all the coaching I had gotten from my stepdad, and all the hard knocks of hockey that had taught me to persevere—they all kicked in at the same time. I won't say I wasn't angry. I was: mostly mad at myself for getting into this jam in the first place. But I used that anger to add to the resolve that welled up in me. I was going to get out of this. In a few hours, I'd be sitting in front of a fire, warm and dry even as the storm raged on outside the door. This was going to be a great story to tell my friends. A night alone in the wilderness.

IF I COULDN'T get out of this bowl by walking, I told myself as I stood staring at the circular tracks I'd made, then I'd have to ride out. It was after seven now, and I was surrounded by darkness and plunging snow. But I had no choice. I would climb back to where I made my first run and try it again, this time concentrating on keeping up my momentum and building up enough speed to bring me out the other side.

I started the climb back up the slope, using my board as an anchor in the snow, pounding it in and then pulling myself along. However difficult my trek through the valley had been, it was nothing compared to the sheer energy I had to expend to get back up that hill. To help focus my efforts and keep myself pumped, I pulled out my MP3 and stuck in the earplugs. I had earlier programmed a batch of songs for what I thought was going to be my last run of the day. Among them were some live tracks from Pearl Jam, along with such Eminem cuts as "Business" and "Say What You Say." I played them all, but the one I kept coming back to over and over as I made that slow ascent was Eminem's "Soldier."

"I'm a soldier," he rapped behind a powerful bass line, *"these shoulders hold up so much. They won't budge, I'll never fall or fold up. I'm a soldier, even if my collar bones crush or crumble, I will never slip or stumble."*

I had what I felt was a special connection to that song. During my second college hockey game, my own collarbone had been snapped. "Soldier" became my theme song during that climb, its rhythm matched to my own pounding heart. I was a soldier, too, and I was never going to fall or fold up, no matter how rough things got.

After about an hour of intense work, I had only made it to about halfway up to the point of my original run. I decided to give it another shot from that point, hoping I had come up far enough and would gain enough speed to make it through the bowl this time. I turned off the music. I need to concentrate now, and in the total silence that enveloped me I felt the first rush of real fear. I knew now what I was up against. It was so dark I could hardly see my hand in front of my face. The snow and fog cut my visibility even more. Somehow I was going to have to make it down that slope fast enough to bring me to the far ridge. But I was already beginning at a disadvantage, having only made it half as far as I'd started out, while the danger of hitting trees on my way down was just as real as ever. I would try to follow my previous tracks, if I could even see them, hoping to stay inside my own turns to increase my downward speed. But what I was about to attempt was going to be extremely dangerous no matter what route I took. One slight miscalculation and I'd slam into a tree trunk, knocking myself unconscious or worse.

I took a deep breath and launched myself. The next few minutes was a hair-raising thrill ride that tested my skills to the max. More than once I felt the solid bulk of a tree pass within inches of me and I was almost knocked down when branches whipped me in the face and body. Luckily I could actually feel the tracks I had made earlier underneath my board and was able to gain significantly more speed, considering the short slope I had started on.

But in the end it wasn't enough. Once again I ground to a halt, not more than a hundred and fifty feet from where I'd last stopped. I immediately sank back up to my thighs in the snow and just stood there for a moment, trying to process what had happened. I could hear the rustling of the wind in the pine needles, and although the storm still loomed over me, I detected the faint trace of moonlight reflected off the snow with a ghostly luminosity. It was as if my senses had suddenly become extraordinarily acute. I had a supersensitivity to my surroundings, a survival instinct that heightened my awareness. It was an attentiveness that would only grow as time went on.

It was becoming clear to me that I wasn't going to make it out of the snowbound bowl until morning. It was another good twist in the tale I would tell my friends. I needed light to see where I was going if I wanted to either hike out or make another attempt at riding through the forest. I was stuck here for the night, cold and hungry but never doubting that I was going to extricate myself sooner or later. At that point I just had to accept the fact that it was going to be later.

I moved deeper into the trees, looking for a place to hunker down. At the base of a large trunk, I found some exposed roots and dug around them until I had hollowed out a space that would provide shelter from the wind that had been whipping up periodically since the sun went down. My next move was to use the sharp edge of my board to strip away some bark and leaves as padding for my lair and to keep me from direct contact with the snow. I settled in, pulling my jacket up over my head and tucking my legs into my chest. As I tried to get as comfortable as possible for the long night ahead, I felt a slight bulge in one of the outside pockets of the jacket. As I unzipped it and dug inside, my heart skipped a beat. A small baggie held half a dozen wooden matches. I almost shouted out loud with joy and relief. The Ripzone I was wearing was one of the first snowboarding parkas I'd ever bought, almost five years previously. Sometime back then, I'd stashed away these matches, maybe in anticipation of smoking a little pot while I was on the slopes. I actually didn't remember when or why I'd put them there. Not that it mattered. With a fire, I could stay warm and dry. My luck was finally turning.

I scavenged around my nest until I found twigs and leaves dry enough that they might actually light. To improve my chances, I took off my cap and pulled out wool strands with my teeth to help kindle the fire. Then I opened the baggie and this time my heart sank. I could feel dampness clinging to the inside of the plastic. After five years in that same pocket, the seam of the baggie had split and let in moisture. Even the paper striker I had put in was soggy.

With trembling hands I pulled out a match. Hardly able to see which end was which, I felt for the tip. It disintegrated in my fingers. With painstaking care I took out another one and tried to strike it. There wasn't even a fizzle. One after the other I attempted to ignite the wet matches until, with a rising sense of desperation, I came to the last one. For twenty minutes I held it in my hands, hoping my body warmth would dry it out. Before I took my last shot, I tried to improve my odds by adding little shreds of my T-shirt to the tepee fire that I had prepared. A thread got caught between my teeth, where it would stay, a constant irritant, from then on.

The colder I got, the more I clung to the idea that the last match would flare to life if I just gave it enough time to dry. Finally, when I couldn't stand the suspense or the cold any longer, I took it out and tried to strike it. It broke in half and I just held on to the stump of wood, not quite able to believe that my last chance for warmth was gone.

A deep chill was slowly spreading over my body. The fact that I had taken off my gloves and tucked them against my skin under my armpits didn't help. I had to keep them pressed against me, cold and clammy and adding to my general misery. In the back of my mind was the worrisome thought that my feet were also wet, and shriveled and pruned. I knew that if I spent the night there, not moving, there was a good chance they would freeze. Suddenly the option of staying put didn't seem quite so practical. As much as anything, it was the incredible darkness and silence that was beginning to get to me. No one knew where I was, or that I was even missing. The enormous expanse of the wilderness around me seemed to suddenly press in, a suffocating, claustrophobic feeling. I needed to do something to make a move. It was part of the meth mentality that had warped my thinking for so long. I just needed to keep moving. It was as if the drug wouldn't let me stop, take a deep breath, and consider the situation. If I had, I would have stayed put. But in that moment, anything was better than just sitting there in a hole, slowly freezing to death.

CHAPTER FIVE

The Valley of the Shadow of Death

I KNEW NOW that I wasn't going to be able to simply ride or hike back into the resort. My fruitless attempts had already proved beyond any doubt that I really was beyond the edge. As I climbed out of my hole and prepared to strike out again, I carefully weighed my options. Since getting back in bounds, where I could ride down a groomed slope to the base of the mountain, was impossible, my only other choice was to move *out* of bounds. I knew that below me to the east was a lodge that had been built outside the perimeter of the ski boundaries. It was called Tamarack Lodge and it became my new destination and the intense focus of my attention. Even though I'd never been there, I had a clear picture of it in my mind: warm and inviting, with a buffet table and a hot tub to soak away the memories of the past several hours.

Instead of heading left now, I took off toward the right, and I hadn't pushed very far through the drifts of snow before I came to a slope that marked the eastern edge of the Dragon's Back bowl that had trapped me. There was a steep slope here that cut even farther into the unmarked limits of the mountain, and I got a real sense of satisfaction by riding it down as far as I could, carefully avoiding trees but still trying to maintain as much speed as possible. Even though I was traversing uncharted territory, it felt good to be moving again instead of crouched in a freezing hole trying to light wet matches.

It was pitch dark and impossible to see more than a few feet ahead of where I was going. I made two or three sharp turns to avoid trees, trying to keep myself pointed in the general direction of where I felt Tamarack was. The slope eventually leveled out and I hiked another hundred yards or so until I came to the next drop. This one was even steeper, and as I launched myself off I suddenly heard a very disconcerting sound. The bottom of my board was scraping along something sharp and hard—rocks or fallen trees or a combination of both. Whatever it was, the snow pack wasn't sticking to it, and I had a vertiginous vision of approaching a cliff too steep to hold on to the heavy fall of the storm. I felt as if I were riding along the spine of a ridge that would soon end in a sharp drop to oblivion. I knew that sound only too well. Sometimes on a fast run I would pass over the trunks of fallen trees, riding them like a skateboarder rides a rail. It was the same grinding sensation that I was getting now, only this time I had no idea what was underneath me or how long it was going to be there.

As I later found out, I was traversing straight for Hangman's Cliff, a famed summer climbing spot for expert grapplers.

I had no choice but to slow down, and through a combination of short rides and slogging along on foot, I managed to keep myself going forward. As I hesitantly proceeded I thought to myself, *This is the steepest terrain you've ever faced.* I could only hope it was in the right direction. I remembered what had happened earlier, how I'd moved steadily in one direction only to discover that I had circled back on myself. I couldn't be sure I wasn't doing the same thing this time. I got a bit of reassurance when I stumbled on a sign almost buried in the snow. It had an octagonal shape, which meant that it was marking the outside perimeter of the ski boundaries. At least I was pointed in the general direction I needed to go.

There was simply no way I could get or keep my bearing in the thick darkness of that night and the even thicker snow that obliterated any landmark that might have helped me to navigate. I was effectively blind, groping toward the mirage of Tamarack that I had pictured so vividly in my mind's eye. As the midnight hours wore on, I tried everything I could to keep myself on course. If I felt as if a turn on a slope had taken me too far to the west, I'd adjust myself back to the east. When I pushed through the snow, I tried to keep myself oriented in as straight a line as possible.

It was futile. Even though the snow wasn't falling quite as heavily and I had slightly better visibility, there was nothing in front or behind that could help me to get my bearings. I was pretty much exhausted from the exertions I'd been making steadily for the last three or four hours, and I was beginning to feel pangs of hunger. I kept expecting the lights of Tamarack to appear over the next rise or down the next valley, and I kept getting disappointed. There was nothing to do but keep pushing on.

Then, as I climbed over a small rise, there was a break in the clouds and a pale sliver of moon shone through to reveal a wide, snowbound vista in front of me. I felt a shiver go down my spine and this time it wasn't from the freezing air or my soggy feet. I knew now that Tamarack wasn't going to be over the next hill or through the next stand of trees. Tamarack was a long way off. I had arrived at the far side of the mountain, at least two or three miles from where I wanted to be. I hadn't walked in a circle. Instead, I had made my way around the bulk of Mammoth to the opposite flank of the park. I knew where I was now. And it was the last place I wanted to be.

The moonlit landscape had an eerie and unreal quality. A softly undulating field of snow was dotted with what looked like jagged black daggers, twenty feet high and pointed to the sky. They extended off to the horizon, sentinels in a place where no human belonged. I felt as if I had stumbled onto an Indian burial ground or some sort of ancient site of ritual sacrifice, deathly still and haunted by uneasy ghosts. But I knew exactly what I was looking at: the burnt-out stumps of trees from a forest fire that had ravaged this side of the mountain two years previously. It had been a serious blaze and I remembered hearing about it from the townspeople down in Mammoth, who had pointed out to me where the flames had consumed the thick stands of old-growth pine. I no longer had to wonder where I was. It was as far from warmth and food and safety as I could possibly have strayed.

I stood there, chest high in snow, grappling with the realization that I was going to have to turn around and retrace my steps back to where I'd started. That awareness quickly brought another: I didn't have the reserves of energy I would need to return, much less make it to Tamarack that night. Like it or not, I was going to have to find shelter in this unearthly place.

At that moment, I recalled something I hadn't thought about in years. I didn't have a religious background. My family didn't go to church and we certainly didn't study the Bible. But I had heard a scriptural passage somewhere and it came back to me as clearly as a voice crying out in the wilderness. It was Psalm 23, the verse that reads, "Yea, though I walk through the shadow of the valley of death, I shall fear no evil." There was no doubt in my mind as I looked out across the charred remnants of that forest pointing up like dead fingers into the heavens that

I had arrived in the valley of death. But it was hard to fear no evil and I felt a trembling in my exhausted body. Whether it was from the cold or from dread of being in that place, I had no way of knowing. And it didn't much matter.

I WAS BREATHING heavily, partly from struggling through the snow for so long and partly from the impact of knowing now just how remote my chances were of making it off the mountain that night. Despite the fact that I was cold and wet and tired, I was going to have to stay put until there was enough light to see where I was going. There was no other option. I didn't like it, but that's what it had come to.

I wasted a few minutes berating myself for the carelessness that had gotten me into this situation in the first place. I knew better. I knew this mountain, the terrain and the conditions, as well if not better than most. I had plenty of experience with winter weather and knew the precautions and safety measures that were critical in keeping yourself together. Instead, it had all come apart. I called myself every name I could think of for the lapse of common sense that had sent me out the door that day so ill-prepared. I had no one to blame but me, and I wasn't about to let myself off the hook.

But it wasn't long before I ran out of self-recrimination. Even now, miles from civilization, stuck in a nightmarish spot totally exposed to the elements, I never once doubted that I'd be telling this tale to the boys in the locker room after a men's league game. It was simply inconceivable to me that I had gotten myself deeper into danger than I could get out of on my own. I still had supreme faith in my ability, both physical and mental, to prevail, no matter how adverse the circumstances.

And right now my circumstance was hunger. I felt the rumbling in my stomach, prompting me suddenly to remember the four pieces of Bazooka bubble gum I had taken with me that morning. Pulling two of them out of my pocket, I chewed eagerly until the sweet flavor was gone and then promptly swallowed them. In my heightened state of awareness, I could actually feel the slight rush of sugar combining with the traces of meth still in my bloodstream and together giving a short, sharp burst of energy. I crumpled up the wrappers and put them back in my pocket. I may have been lost in the wilderness, but I wasn't about to let myself become a litterbug.

Then, from the corner of my eye, I saw something move. I turned and squinted through the mist that was coming up off the ground now that the snow had lightened to a gentle fall. I saw their eyes first, a yellow unblinking stare as they moved stealthily through the drifts. Two wolves. As I watched them stalk me, it was clear that this was their territory and that they were in their element. They moved effortlessly through the snow, built to hunt and kill in these very conditions. In comparison, I felt like a bowling ball trying to roll through sand. I was awkward and oafish and pretty much defenseless if they chose to attack. I was on their turf and I was playing by their rules—the ruthless rules of the wilderness.

As unnerving as it was to see two wild animals moving toward me, cautious but relentless, I was in for an even more jarring surprise when I sensed something behind me and I turned to find a third wolf inches away and sniffing at the gum in my pocket. A cold rush of sheer terror shot through me. I grasped my board and held it up close to my body like a shield, at the same time letting out a yell that echoed across the expanse.

I had never encountered an animal as dangerous or de-termined as a wolf before, but from somewhere I had dredged up a scrap of advice about how to defend myself: make yourself as large and as loud as possible. I knew that wolves hunted in packs and that these three-to-one odds were not in my favor unless I could somehow intimidate them and frighten them off. It wasn't hard to act totally freaked out, roaring at the top of my lungs and making the sounds of a cracking whip and waving my arms like a wind-mill. I *was* freaked out. And for good reason. A few weeks before my ordeal, a skier had also gotten lost on the moun-tain. When they found him two weeks later, all that was left were a pair of gnawed legs. For these predators, hu-mans were fair game.

Without waiting to see if my display of aggression had worked, I took off as fast as I could, laboring through the snow, still shouting and whipping my arms in every direction. My fight-or-flight instinct was fully cranked. The proximity of that third wolf had given me a burst of adrenaline that kept me pumping through the waist-high drifts, convinced that it was right behind me and ready to pounce. I was completely panicked, hardly able to catch my breath. All I wanted now was to put as much distance between me and those vicious fangs as I could, and I pushed my way through with every ounce of strength until I came to a large scorched tree trunk and collapsed into the snow. I braced my board in front of me and, panting for air, waited for the attack I knew was coming.

Seconds passed, then minutes. The silence was almost as frightening as an animal's snarl would have been, but I was slowly able to get a grip on myself and try and figure out my next move. The first thing I wanted to do was to get something solid behind my back. I had the vivid image of the wolves crouching down to leap at me from the rear, so I hollowed out another burrow in the snow, digging right up against the blackened wood. This time I didn't bother looking for bark or leaves to feather my nest. I was relieved just to be in a hold surrounded on three sides.

I could still hear that third wolf sniffing at my pockets, which made me think that the odor of the bubble gum must have been strong enough to attract them. I yanked out the two remaining pieces and threw them as far as I could in either direction, doing the same with the crumpled wrappers, forgetting for the moment about leaving trash behind. For good measure, I took off my gloves and rubbed them against the tree, trying to eradicate the smell of the gum. It occurred to me that, after a day of sweating profusely, I probably smelled as pungent as the Bazooka, but there was nothing I could do about that.

I settled back in my hole with my board at the ready to shield against any lunging carnivores, but I still didn't feel secure. Far from it. I continued to push up the snow to make a barrier around me, but what I really needed was a weapon. Looking around the little sanctuary I had constructed, I found a sturdy branch protruding from the tree and only slightly scorched. I broke it off, dug my board into the snow, and for the next few hours used the graphite edge to whittle out a dagger. As time dragged on, the knife became more elaborate. I even managed to carve a scabbard and finger grips, all the time muttering and whispering, trying to give myself the reassurance and encouragement I needed to make it through the night. The knife would be sharp enough, I repeated over and over. If they came at me and I managed to kill one of them, it would scare the others off. I was going to make it. I just needed to hang on until daylight. A little longer. A little longer.

I had never felt more exposed and vulnerable in my life. The self-confidence that had carried me through so much was under siege, and I could feel my defenses slipping. The panic that I had experienced at the sight of the wolf pack had now turned into a grim obsession. I put all the tension and anxiety I was grappling with into carving my dagger, which came to represent my only protection against the vast and hostile world that was bearing down on me. My state of mind wasn't helped by the vestiges of the meth that had been circulating in my system for so long, combined with periodic jolts of adrenaline that coursed through my body and even the fading effects of the sugar from the bubble gum. I desperately needed sleep, but was too cold and edgy to even close my eyes.

By now I was plunged into the darkest hour just before the dawn, maybe 4 a.m., although I had no way of knowing for sure. It had finally stopped snowing, but what had already fallen acted as a giant muffler, damping down any sound. It was as quiet as a tomb and I stopped carving long enough to listen to the absolute silence, so deep I imagined I could hear my own breath expelled from my lungs and the blood pumping through my veins.

Then, from what seemed like a great distance, came a soft but persistent moan. It got closer and closer until I was hit with a blast of wind like an artic scythe. I'd been cold before but there was nothing to compare to the way that howling wind cut into my very bones. It slackened for a moment before I heard it coming again, louder this time, like a freight train bearing down. Sweeping over me, it blew snow crystals into my face like shards of glass.

I pulled myself into my jacket, zipping it up over my head and drawing my arms out of the sleeves, still manically carving the wood from inside. Every few minutes I'd unzip myself far enough to peer out and look around, then

quickly huddle back inside my meager protection. The
jacket had a hood, but not like the airtight ones that more
heavy-duty parkas would feature, fur lined with a draw-
string that cinches up tight around your face. So I pulled
up my goggles around my head to help clamp down the
hood and kept whittling away. It wasn't long before I began to feel an uncomfortable itching on my arms and
abdomen. I flashed back to my pro hockey days, when
players would shave down their stick shafts and blades for
better feel with more blade surface on the ice. The saw-
dust and wood splinters would get lodged in our clothing
and rub against our skin. We even had a name for it: the
Gunk. Now, from hacking away at that branch for hours,
I'd gotten myself gunked.

I was beginning to wonder what else could possibly
happen to me, when I noticed that I was starting to get a
little light-headed. The reason was simple: huddled inside
my jacket, I was slowly suffocating. It took me a few minutes to work out a solution. With the wind still howling
around me, I extended the sleeves of the jacket, hooking
the cuffs to the mounts or bindings on my board. I now
had two air passages and carefully inhaled a fresh breath
through one and expelled it through the other. I alter-
nated with a regular rhythm, still listening intently between the gusts of wind, waiting to hear the soft crunch of
snow that would signal the return of the wolves.

That's what kept me occupied through the waning
hours of the night. I had forgotten now about the fear of

my feet freezing if I didn't keep moving. All that mattered now was to stay as still as possible, to preserve my body heat inside my flimsy cocoon with its jerry-rigged air vents. I tried to close my eyes and coax out a few minutes of sleep, but every time I did, a vivid image of the vastness all around rose up to overwhelm me, and my lids snapped back open.

But in the end I must have slipped off. It might have been a half hour, maybe a little more. All I knew was that when my eyes popped open again, the first wan light of dawn was leaking through the thin fabric that encased me like a shroud.

CHAPTER SIX

The Baggie

I CLIMBED OUT of my makeshift snow bunker on the second morning on the mountain to find a thick layer of damp fog clinging to the landscape, reducing visibility to fifteen feet at the outside. I could see part of the trail I had made the night before, marking my ragged and meandering progress to nowhere. It looked like some large animal in its death throes had passed by. I studied the slope carefully for signs of wolf tracks.

The temperature seemed to have dropped even further, but as difficult as it was to tolerate the freezing cold, it was thirst that was my main concern.

I was beginning to feel the effects of dehydration, despite the fact that I had tried to slake my need for water by eating snow. Ironically, the first night I had arrived at the condo I had found a book about surviving in the wilderness and had passed a few hours glancing through it. Some of the material I had read there I was now facing firsthand.

I knew that, sooner rather than later, I was going to need real liquid. The snow not only had the effect of making me colder, but it did nothing to diminish the physical craving for water. In fact, eating too much snow or ice can contribute to general dehydration, by increasing sensitivity to cold. It also impairs the shivering response, which is an essential way the body generates heat in frigid conditions. Eating snow can eventually sap your energy, which only adds to the adverse effects of prolonged exposure. The bottom line was, I needed water, real water. Without it, I wouldn't be able to maintain myself for long.

Despite the heavy mist that clung to the ground, I was able to make out a small ascent not far from my burrow. It was situated in such a way that if I could get to the top I could ride it down back in the direction I had come and work my way over to the front of Mammoth. I strapped on my board again and launched into the surreal backdrop of burned trees and snowdrifts, a study in stark black and white.

I had to be especially careful about the path I took through the charred stumps. It was only too easy to imagine a wrong turn that would end up with me impaled on one of those sharp stakes. As it was, fallen trunks occasionally appeared out of nowhere, forcing me to ollie up and over them by leaning back and springing over the obstruction. It was difficult and demanding, but it was also more than a little exhilarating. At least I was on the move again, taxing my skills in conditions that tested the limits of my stamina. But I had the memory of the wolves and my own growing thirst to spur me on.

I made my way to another small hill and went for another all-too-brief ride. When I stopped, I took out my cell phone and, as I had done a few times during the previous night, turned it on in hopes of picking up a signal. I tried to ignore the rapidly shrinking battery icon in the corner of the screen as I dialed 911 and listened. Nothing. I'd only be able to try reaching help a few more times before I ran out of juice. I carefully turned it off and put it back in my jacket pocket. Even if I wasn't going to use it again that day, there was something comforting about knowing that there was still a little life preserved in the circuitry. As much as anything, the cell phone battery had become a measure of the hope I had in trying to keep alive. Whether or not I actually got a signal seemed less important than the fact that there was still a possibility of getting through, as long as the battery didn't die completely.

As my heavy breathing subsided, the silence of the valley enveloped me. There was still the sense of awe and wonder within these pathless woods. The fog hung like thick drapes all around me, muffling every sound and making me strain to listen for what might be the noise of an approaching chopper or the shouts of the ski patrol looking for me. But instead, all I heard was the soft rushing whisper that seemed to be originating from down the hill. Considering my thirst, I wondered if it might be an aural hallucination, but after a moment, I was convinced that it was the real thing: there was water somewhere in close proximity.

Soon I emerged onto a broad slope that was marked with strange, elongated figure-eight patterns. They seemed to have been scored into the snow. I had no idea what could have made them. I found out soon enough, as I stepped over one and it immediately collapsed underneath me. The figure eights had been carved by runoffs from the slopes into a nearby river, which had then been covered over and hidden by the wind-blown snow. There was a hollow space anywhere from six to eight feet deep between the water and the drift that had hardened over it, and when I had set my weight down, the crust of snow had given way.

Fortunately, I had been carrying my snowboard behind me, so that when I broke through the snow dome my fall was, in turn, blocked by the board. It actually held me up and I hung suspended over the rocks and rivulets. I stared down at my dangling feet and realized suddenly just how many unexpected dangers lurked in this pristine wilderness, this strange realm where no man intrudes. I could have easily fallen all the way through and snapped a bone or sprained an ankle. I had to be a lot more cautious from now on.

Aided by a rush of adrenaline, I was able to haul myself out of the hole and use the board to maneuver inch by inch back to solid ground. I lay in the snow and closed my eyes. I had a feeling of accomplishment: I'd saved myself from injury or even death. But that sense of satisfaction was immediately followed by the realization of how far I'd sunk in so short a time. It wasn't all that long ago that I'd considered myself a conqueror of mountains, seeking out the most difficult and dangerous trails to test my skills against the untamed wild.

Now here I was, congratulating myself for not falling into a hole, knowing that it was only luck—the simple fact that I had been carrying my board behind me—that had quite possibly save my life. In the darkness behind my eyelids, I realized just how small and insignificant I was, a speck in a featureless world of white. I was lost in that void and it was only later that I came to find out that I had wandered nine miles, some of it in circles, from my starting point.

MY THOUGHTS WERE wandering into those ever-tightening circles, as well, returning again and again to both self-recrimination for getting myself into this situation and relief that I hadn't made it worse by breaking a leg. But it wasn't long before my overriding concern began to reassert itself. The sound of running water was much closer now and with it my thirst returned with a vengeance. Getting up, I made my way forward, careful now to avoid the treacherous figure eights. In areas where I wasn't sure where I was stepping, I stabbed my board into the snow to be certain that it wouldn't break away. After a few minutes,

I finally came to the banks of a swiftly flowing river some eight feet wide and three to four feet deep.

Setting my board to one side, I ventured out onto the bank, which was really nothing more than a shelf of ice and snow. I had learned my lesson stepping through the fragile snow crust over the runoff from the river. I carefully inched my way along and, when I got close enough to the water, where it ran clean and fresh over the rock, I got down on my hands and knees. Even then I was fearful of putting too much pressure on the frozen crust, so I laid myself out on my stomach, with my face close to the clear rushing water. To stabilize myself in this awkward position, I took off my glove and braced my hand against a rock in the stream. Then I lowered my head and drank, before I figured out I could use my twenty-dollar bill, rolled up, as a straw.

It was like putting fuel in a gas tank. I immediately felt energy surging through my dehydrated cells, an instant, electrifying jolt of renewal that was, at the same time, cleansing and purifying. It was the most refreshing drink I had ever taken. I couldn't get enough and I slurped it up greedily until I had to come up for air. I had closed my eyes to better savor the incredible sensation that was coursing through my body, and when I opened them again, I heard and noticed that a crack had appeared in the ice of the bank. I quickly worked my way back from the edge of the river and, grabbing my board, moved downstream a few yards to where the overhang looked a little sturdier.

Once again I shimmied out on my belly, this time taking my board with me. I drank just as deeply as I had before, and then turned on my back and just lay with my face to the sky, lulled by the sound of the water rushing past my head. It was then that the thought returned to me: *You've got meth.* It was a powerful temptation. Now that I had satisfied my thirst and my fears of dehydration were lessened, I suddenly craved the elation and euphoria that the meth would give me. I would have all the energy I needed to get off the mountain. Those crystals could make me the man I needed to be in a matter of seconds.

I took the baggie out of my pocket and stared for a long moment at the glittering crystals in a pile at the bottom corner of the bag, no bigger than a thumbnail. A quarter of it would do the job. The rest I could save for later, after I had a good night's sleep. It would be my reward for all that I'd gone through for the past few days.

But even as I parceled out the last lines of speed in my imagination, once again something held me back. The Bible talks about "a still small voice" inside of us all, and I can't say for sure whether it was the whisper of my conscience or common sense that I was hearing. My addiction to speed—the way it clouded my judgment and inflated my own delusions of grandeur—had been largely responsible for getting me into this predicament in the first place. It was a fact that I didn't want to admit, but in that moment, it was hard to ignore. For the better part of a year, I had given myself over to a chemical that dictated my choices. Now I was facing a crisis of survival more urgent than anything I'd ever confronted, and it was up to me to make the choices that would help me survive.

I considered whether or not I should take out my meth baggie and use it to give me enough energy to continue my journey. It was a tempting notion. The drug could provide a sustained burst of artificial power and elevate my mood, pumping me up. But I also knew the inevitable downside. I'd be burning fuel I didn't have, pushing myself to unreasonable limits with the false assurance that I could keep going.

What would follow then would be a low, slow comedown that would leave me worse off than I'd begun, exhausted, tense, and paranoid. Of course, by that time, I might have actually found my way off the mountain and would have been able to soak away my aches and pains with a hot tub, a toke of weed, and a couple of drinks—my perfect buzz. But something told me it was a risk I'd better not take. There'd be time enough later, I told myself, to get high. Right now I had to take care of business, which meant taking care of myself.

Help yourself were the words I had read on the inside of my eyelids. If I didn't heed that simple instruction now, if I let speed help me instead, I would be forfeiting the last vestige of my identity. Meth would save me; it would own me; and eventually it would kill me.

At least that's how it seemed as I lay on that frozen riverbank staring up at that fogbound sky, grappling with emotions I'd never had before. It was a unique experience for me to struggle against my own impulses. I'd never really thought much about weighing out the consequences of my own actions. But if the last two days had taught me anything, it was that impulses and actions *do* have consequences. I understood instinctively that what I chose to do next was, literally, a matter of life and death. As I said, I don't know for sure whether the voice I was hearing was coming from some core part of me. Maybe it was God. Maybe it was my grandfather. But whoever it was, I listened. I upended the baggie and watched as the meth sprinkled out onto the water and was washed away like flakes of powdered snow.

A long minute passed as I tried to gauge how I felt. Regret was mixed with relief. Fear of giving up what I had learned to depend on grappled with a rush of newfound self-determination. Part of me wanted to undo what I had done, to bring back the chemical-laden water and swallow it whole. Another part felt proud that, for the first time in as long as I could remember, I was in control of the drug and not the other way around. If I was going to survive this ordeal, I would do it on my own. From here on out it was just the mountain and me. And it was that determination that carried me forward.

Even though the speed was gone, I still had the baggie and I realized at once that it would come in handy. I rinsed it out as best I could and, filling it with water, took another long drink. But there was still a faint taste of meth clinging to the plastic, as if the drug was making one last attempt to hook me back in. I even felt the slightest rush from the traces that had dissolved in the water, and with it came a sharp sting of remorse. I quickly filled the bag again and gulped down the water. I kept repeating the filling and emptying until it almost became a ritual and the sense of desperation faded. I told myself that, while I may have given up the speed, I had gained a valuable tool for survival. I could fill the baggie with snow, let my body temperature melt it, and have a ready supply of water as I continued my trek. That little pouch of plastic was going to keep me alive.

I took a deep breath and laid out my strategy for the rest of the day. Above me was another hill that formed part of the ridgeback. I would climb up to the top and try to get my bearings. Once I got oriented again, I would strike out for Tamarack. There was every chance I would be back at the condo by nightfall.

But I lingered a moment at the edge of the rushing river before gathering my strength and setting out. The sound of the water was immensely soothing and I found myself thinking back to a time when I had gone with some friends to Yosemite on a white-water rafting trip. It had been one of the most enjoyable times I could remember, even though from my vantage point on the riverbank, the experience seemed distant and remote. It was as if it had happened to another person. Yet, at the same time, I felt a stirring of hope. Maybe that person still existed. Maybe I

could reclaim some of the optimism and joy and exuber-
ance that had once characterized my life. Maybe the slow
crystallizing of my spirit could be reversed.

I bent down to get one last drink, reaching my hand
out again to steady myself on a rock. I leaned forward trying to get a firm grip on the wet surface of the stone, and as
I did I heard a sharp cracking sound. The snowbank gave
way and I plunged face-first into the freezing water.

CHAPTER SEVEN

Fire Dance

SHOCKED BY THE plunging glacial cold and gasping for breath, inhaling water, I was immediately dragged into the middle of the river by the swift-running current. For a moment I had no concept of up or down, right or left. I was consumed by the frothing, freezing torrent, as I fought for my bearings.

Still clutching my board, I struggled to right myself, but the water was moving so fast that, even though the river was no more than four feet deep, it was impossible to regain my equilibrium. Instead, I was being dragged along the bottom, my knees and shins colliding with the sharp jagged rocks beneath the water, sending sharp jolts of pain through my stunned body. In a desperate attempt to edge out of the current, I threw up my board to block the water, but the river easily overpowered me and pushed back, sending me reeling downstream even faster, whipping me around until the board was actually dragging me through the current.

At last I was able to get a footing, long enough at least to lodge my board between the rocks and pull myself toward the bank. Fighting with every ounce of strength, I repeated the process, getting a firm wedge that I could use to angle myself through the water one short step at a time. More than once I unknowingly stepped into a deeper section of the river and, plunging chest deep, was dragged along again until I could gain another foothold, sometimes almost paddling my way into a shallower eddy.

Slowly, with agonizing effort, I was able to pull myself to the bank. I collapsed onto the rocky, ice-covered surface, the blood pounding in my ears and my body soaked and numb. I collapsed for a few minutes, waiting for the roaring in my head to subside. But it only got louder. Sitting up, I looked downstream, where, moments before, I was being helplessly dragged. The thundering I heard wasn't in my head after all. It was coming from the seventy-foot drop of a waterfall.

Not far from a spectacular formation of basalt rocks called the Devil's Post Pile, Rainbow Falls is a popular Mammoth Mountain hiking destination during the summer months. There is, in fact, a shuttle bus that takes visitors up to the expanse of Red Meadow when the wildflowers bloom, and the hardiest among the visitors sometimes continue on to the falls. Named for the prism effect formed in the heavy mist, Rainbow Falls is a familiar feature of the region, fed by the waters of the Mammoth Lakes.

I knew all that, of course, from my extensive boarding experience on the mountain. But in that moment, sitting shivering with my feet still in the water, I wasn't able to make the connection. All I knew was that I wasn't more than fifteen feet from a fatal plunge over the edge of a raging waterfall. I doubt it would have made much difference to me even if I had been able to identify my general location. Rainbow Falls was a long way from any ranger station or ski lodge. There was not going to be any bus coming to pick me up; not in the dead of winter. Realizing exactly how far I was from the possibility of rescue might only have brought on a fresh wave of discouragement. All I was really aware of was that, once again, the wilderness had lashed out and almost killed me. I had survived by the skin of my teeth and I didn't know how many more close calls I could endure.

Besides, I was now facing a problem more immediate than identifying the name of the waterfall I had almost been swept over. By the time I had actually reached the bank, I had been taken far down the river from where I had initially fallen in. The gently sloping descent was gone, replaced now by a sheer ice-covered cliff twenty-five feet high, cut through at the base by the torrent of water. There was only one way out and that was straight up.

For the next half hour I undertook one of the most difficult physical challenges of my life. In heavy wet clothes, using only my snowboard for support, I made my way up that cliff face. My progress was measured in inches and every inch required superhuman effort. I had to jam my board as hard as I could into the snow and ice, testing the stability along with trying to secure an anchor to pull myself up. If I couldn't get enough of a purchase in the almost vertical ascent, I would thrust my arm angled downward shoulder-deep into the snow while kicking climbing holes with my boots. More than once my efforts dislodged a spray of snow, and it gave me a knot in my stomach to think that, at any moment, I could trigger an avalanche that could hurl me back down the embankment and into the river again. The whole cliff felt unstable and with every move the risk of bringing down tons of snow on top of me seemed more heightened.

At last I was able to pull myself over the top, where I lay completely spent, the numbness of my body masking the ache in my muscles. I knew that I couldn't lie there for long without risking hypothermia, so I pulled myself together and stood up. Despite the cold, I could now feel the bruises and cuts I had sustained on my legs from being dragged along the river bottom, and my stance was unsteady as I looked out on the plateau where I had arrived.

The ridge I had seen earlier rose above me to the east, but there was no possibility of climbing it to get a better vantage until I did something to improve my situation. My wet clothes were clammy and already beginning to get stiff from freezing. I needed to get them off before they stuck to me. Crossing through the heavy snow, I headed to a tree with low branches that hung over a flat rocky platform. Standing on the rock, I stripped off everything except my boots and hung all of it out on the limbs, hoping that at least some of the moisture would evaporate.

I was naked now, my flesh exposed to the elements. I did what I could to keep warm, rubbing my skin and jumping up and down to stimulate my circulation. After a half hour or so, my movements took on a rhythmical quality and I started chanting. It was a whisper at first, forced out between the white chill of my breath, but then louder and louder until I was actually shouting into the echoing expanse around me. I couldn't form words: I was too cold for that, but the grunts and groans and gibberish spoke volumes. As much as I was trying to keep myself alive and active, I was also yelling out my defiance against nature and the implacable forces that were out to destroy me. I started dancing, shuffling around and throwing my arms from side to side, as if I were a primitive man living in prehistoric times, trying to summon fire from the sky.

It was all a little freaky, but I didn't care. There was no one for miles to see me acting like a fool, and I think the cold was starting to have an effect on my mental state. Whatever it was, it became more and more frenzied until I finally ran out of energy and my dance came to a slow, shambling end. I stood panting as the fading sound of my angry voice accentuated the utter solitude on every side of me. I felt like the last—or the first—man on earth, and I might as well have been. No one was coming to save me. No one knew where I was. No one knew if I was dead or alive, and I wasn't sure which one I was, either. *Help yourself!*

MY CLOTHES, OF course, hadn't dried, despite the fact that a wind had come up and was rustling through the pine needles where my pants, boxers, shirt, and jacket hung on the trees. In hindsight, it probably would have been a better idea to lay them out on the rocks. Whatever heat the stones had absorbed from the sun might have helped to dry them. But I wasn't exactly thinking rationally. The plunge I had taken into the freezing river had left me dazed and confused.

It also turned out that I had totally lost track of time. I got my soggy clothes back on and headed up the ridge, and by the time I arrived at the top, the dimming glow of late afternoon was already darkening the fog draped like a shroud around me. The whole experience I had just been through, from riding down to the river, to my wild dance on the flat rock, seemed to have taken no more than a few hours. In reality I had spent my second full day on the mountain.

I couldn't see more than thirty feet back down the way I had come, but now I realized that the ridgeback I had surmounted extended farther up along a sheer rock face another few hundred or so feet. In the failing light I made my way to a ledge that had been carved by the weather into the ascent and gave me a better view of my immediate surroundings. There was a break in the fog and the first thing I noticed was a stand of trees on the other side of the river, in the direction I had traveled over the course of that trackless day. I peered hard at it, thinking that I saw something unusual among the trunks and boughs of the thick pines. The more I stared, the more certain I became that there was a small ski lift tucked among the trees, the kind used in a tubing park, where kids sit in rubber tires to slide down the mountain.

Logically, of course, it made no sense. I was way outside the bounds of the park and no kiddie lift was going to be operating in this remote location. But that hardly mattered to me. The more I stared at it through the oncoming night, the more convinced I became that it was real. I could see it in every detail and was sure that it would take me to safety if I could only get across the valley and the river that I had just traversed.

I may have been delusional, but even in my impaired state I knew that night would be falling soon, making it impossible to move in the pitch black. No matter what was on the other side of the river, it would have to wait until morning. I was going to have to spend a second night in the wild. I surveyed the ledge I was on, searching for a good spot to settle in for the next twelve hours. A couple hundred feet further along, among a jumble of fallen rocks, I noticed a cave notched into the side of the rock face. It looked like a perfect spot, with boulders on either side of an entrance hole large enough for me to crawl into.

I started to make my way toward it, but then stopped
short. An image had flashed in my mind, one of hibernat-
ing grizzly bears who wouldn't take kindly to the intrusion
of a strange shivering creature. The yellow eyes of the
wolves from the night before were still fresh in my memory, and the longer I looked at the cave, the more vivid the
specter of wild animals with ravenous appetites became. It
was too perfect a shelter not to have already been occupied. As much as I yearned for the feeling of being surrounded by strong and sturdy walls, I reluctantly backed
away. The risk was just too great.

Instead, I scurried away and got busy hacking down
more branches from the scraggly trees clinging to the rock
outcroppings. When I had gathered enough to lie down
on, I dug out a narrow trench on the ledge and spread
them out. It was twilight now, and I settled into my nest to
wait for dark. A light dusting of snow began to fall, then
slowly began to get heavier. I could hear the creak of the
swaying trees, the wind blowing off chunks of snow from
the branches.

"Hello?" I shouted. "Anyone there?" Who could be
making those sounds?

As on the previous night, I could also hear the wind
approaching from what seemed to be miles off, and when
it hit, there was a slam against the side of the ridgeback
like the slap of a giant hand. I drew down deeper into the
branches, ignoring the uncomfortable prickling itch of
the pine needles. It was gratifying to be hearing those an-

gry gusts of wind instead of feeling them directly and to watch the snow being blown over the top of the rock face that was protecting me. I was learning, slowly but surely, how to take care of myself in this unforgiving place.

For a while I was able to occupy my mind with planning my moves for the next morning. I was looking forward to riding back down the valley toward where I was sure I had spied the lift that I was convinced was adjacent to Tamarack. It would be an easy run and I'd be back in time for a big breakfast. But as the night bore down, bringing with it a heavy enveloping darkness, my doubts began to grow. Had I really seen what I thought I'd seen? Was I going to get to safety tomorrow or would I die on this godforsaken ledge, frozen solid or gutted by a voracious predator?

More than anything, I started to experience an acute loneliness. All the bravado of my fire dance earlier in the day had vanished. I longed to hear another human voice, to see a face I knew and one that knew me. Being alone was a much different test of my determination to survive than anything I'd yet experienced. I had been a loner for so long, trapped inside my private world of meth, and now what I wanted more than anything was the warmth of human companionship.

As I lay huddled on my bed of branches, I remembered Tom Hanks and his great role in the movie *Cast Away*. It didn't seem so far-fetched to me that he had developed a relationship with Wilson, the volleyball. I was beginning to feel the same way about my snowboard,

Burton. It had, literally, saved my life on more than one occasion. It was constantly by my side, ready as a tool, a
weapon, and a shield. It was just a hunk of graphite, but in
the solitude of that night, it was also my closest friend.

I don't remember sleeping much on that ledge, but I
must have dozed off a few times because I have a vivid recall of nightmares that frightened me almost as much as
anything the wilderness had thrown at me. Once, in the
dead of the night, I found myself on a vast field of snow,
with the sun blazing brightly overhead. I was terrified that
I would get snow blindness, which I'd experienced a few
times on the slopes to a mild degree. The rays of the sun
can glare so brightly off the snow that it actually blacks
out your vision. In my dream state it seemed to me that,
after everything I'd already gone through, all that was left
to endure was blindness. Before I woke, it seemed to me
that I was staring at my reflection in a mirror, screaming at
the horrific image of my hollowed eye sockets.

My fevered state was, of course, a combination of dehydration, sleep deprivation, and an increasingly severe altitude sickness that left me with a pounding headache.
But I was also struggling against feeling like a victim, vulnerable and defenseless, and looking back, I think the
only way those emotions could express themselves was
through my dreams.

In truth, I was bitterly disappointed. I had fully expected to be back at the condo by now, soaking my bones
and sipping a cold Coca-Cola. I had an acute craving for

sweets, which I attributed to coming down off speed and needing a sugar rush as a substitute. But more than food, I yearned to be in a hot tub. It was a craving that occurred time and again during my ordeal, and that night I fantasized freely about it. I could almost feel the way the water lapped against my skin, and the supremely comforting sensation that came from looking out the window at the cold and forbidding landscape from the warmth and safety of your own personal womb. It was delicious to contemplate, which only made it worse when a sudden gust of wind or the rustling of trees roused me from my reverie and reminded me of where I really was.

Just before dawn I fell asleep again, but this time my nightmare was etched not in white snow, but in utter black. I dreamed that my eyes were shut and, no matter how hard I tried, I couldn't pry them open. For all I know, I was actually staring into the darkness that was all around me, but when I was jerked from sleep by the sound of my own muffled cry, what occurred to me was both the contrast and the similarity between my two dreams. In one it was whiteness that had robbed me of my vision. In the other it was blackness. In both I was deeply and profoundly blind.

After waking for the last time that night, I lay and waited for dawn. Tomorrow I would be off this mountain. This was going to be the end of it, I promised myself. It was time to do or to die. "It was time to get busy living or to get busy dying."

CHAPTER EIGHT

Help Yourself

AS SOON AS there was enough light to see my hand in front of my face, I got out of my rough-and-ready bed and quickly made my way to the promontory where, the night before, I had first seen what I was convinced was a ski lift. The day had dawned cloudy and overcast, but at least the fog had lifted enough to give me a hazy view of the valley below.

If I had felt the pangs of disappointment the previous day, they were nothing compared with the anguished frustration that greeted me that morning. It was immediately evident that what I had seen as a ski lift was nothing more than an optical illusion combined with a lot of wishful thinking. The towlines and T-bars I had delineated were nothing more than a random accumulation of branches and tree trunks. By the first light of morning, I couldn't even make out what I had imagined I'd seen. There was no trace left of the mirage I'd created in my mind.

With a groan I sank down into the snow. One more avenue of escape had been closed off to me. I had to come up with another plan and I had no idea what that might be. It took a long time for the anger and despair I felt to subside and for my head to clear enough for a new plan to begin to emerge. At last I gathered myself together and sat back up to make a careful study of the topography spread out below me. Since there was going to be no quick ride down to civilization or a ski lift, I would have to go back to Plan A and try to find Tamarack Lodge.

I knew I had wandered off track onto the far side of the mountain. Thinking back to the river and my near-death experience of the day before, I finally realized that the cascade I had almost gone over had to be Rainbow Falls. With that as a signpost, I mentally redrew a map of the area and found my approximate position. To the best of my calculations, I estimated the direction of the lodge. It had to be farther east down the valley. Nothing else made sense. It would be a long and difficult hike, especially considering that the ridge on this side of the mountain was steep and remote. But I had no choice. Even if I was wrong in my reckoning, I had run out of other options. I had to trust my best guess and go with it all the way. Whether the decision was good or bad, it was the freedom of choice that mattered in that moment.

I prepared to head back down the valley, carefully fitting my gloves and goggles and bending down to strap myself onto the board. But before I slipped my feet into the bindings, I stopped. Now was the time to face what I dreaded the most. Somewhere in the depths of the previous night, I had tried to wiggle my toes to gauge their condition. While the rest of my body was generally numb, there was no feeling at all below my ankles. I considered, right then and there, taking off my boots to make an evaluation, but it was too dark and I was too cold to follow through. I had promised myself that I would take a close look at my feet in the morning. Now that moment had come and I realized, with a sinking sensation in the pit of my stomach, that I really didn't want to know what I was about to find out.

Taking a deep breath, I sat down on a nearby rock and slipped off my right boot. Underneath, I felt my sock, stiff and unyielding, frozen to my foot. I carefully peeled it back, but when I tried to slide it past my instep it held fast. I clutched my foot in both hands, rubbing it and trying to loosen the grip of the ice that had built up between my skin and the fabric of the sock. Gingerly I tried to free it again, and as I did, I felt a slight stinging pain. I pulled once more and the sock came free. Along with it was a long strip of my own flesh.

Fear rose up in me as I stared at the gruesome sight, trying to process what had happened. Even worse than my skin peeling off was the fact that I had felt hardly anything as it was stripped away from the arch of my foot. It was instantly clear that a layer of my epidermis was simply and irretrievably dead. With a growing sense of dread, I took off my other boot. I managed to get my left sock off, losing even more skin and causing my foot, badly swollen and discolored dark purple, to bleed.

I took the pieces of shredded, bloody skin and wrapped them between two leaves. Even now, my instinct for survival was becoming acute and it occurred to me that I could use my flesh as bait to possibly trap an animal. Nothing, I was coming to realize, could afford to be wasted.

Technically speaking, my feet were frostbitten, but that's just a simple name for a complex and frightening physiological process. It begins after a prolonged exposure to cold, when your body sends signals to your extremities—your hands and feet, your ears and nose—to slow the flow of blood by constricting your vessels. It's a natural and necessary response. Blood is needed to keep vital organs functioning, and by exposing less blood to external cold, you are preventing a further decrease in your internal body temperature. If you get any colder, your brain will permanently constrict the blood flow to keep you from getting hypothermia. When that happens, ice crystals form and water is lost from the cells, causing them to die from dehydration. Holes appear in the vessel walls and blood leaks into the tissues, inflaming them. It's this damage and the resultant clotting that blocks circulation.

Frostbite victims report experiencing a burning and tingling in their affected extremities. Eventually, however, as the cells perish, they go completely numb. It's at that point that they swell up and turn from yellow to bluish-purple. Unless the process is reversed, they usually become gangrenous and, without being removed, the gangrene can spread to the rest of the body with poisonous infection.

In many ways, frostbite can be compared to the effects of meth. The drug causes blood vessels to constrict, cutting off the steady flow of blood to various parts of the body. Your vessels are weakened and destroyed and tissue becomes prone to damage, inhibiting the body's ability to repair itself.

As I sat staring at my already severely swollen injured feet, it was that comparison that flashed through my mind. My mind, my spirit, my life had become crystallized through drug use. What had happened figuratively was now happening literally.

Horrified, I did my best to wring out my wet socks. But before I could even accomplish that simple task, I fell back into the snow, staring up at the steel gray sky.

"You're not as tough as you think you are," I whispered to myself. It might have seemed like an obvious fact: there I was, at the mercy of winter, hunger, and thirst, not to mention wild animals and all the other treacherous pitfalls of an untamed wild. Yet what I was finally able to admit to myself had all the stunning force of a revelation in my mind. All my life I had been taught to be tough and totally self-reliant. It was that lesson that my grandfather had passed along. It was the same lesson that my stepfather and Coach Kyle had drilled into me in game after game. In fact, there was something familiar about the feel of wet socks on my feet, and I suddenly remembered back to my college days, after a game we played very badly. After riding for three hours home on the "Iron Horse," the team bus, the coach angrily ordered us to suit up in our uniforms again and hit the ice for a grueling workout. I could vividly recall the same clammy feel of that sweat-soaked gear and, for a moment, felt grateful for the coach's hard-assed attitude. I may not have been as tough as I thought I was, but I learned the hard way how to endure tough times.

Yet suddenly, now, all the willpower and resolve in the world wouldn't make any difference. I was going to *lose* my feet.

"I'm going to lose my feet," I said, repeating the thought out loud. I sat bolt upright and, reaching out, grabbed my frostbitten feet in my hands. Suddenly there seemed to be nothing more precious, more prized and valued. Blinded by tears, I looked out across the valley and shouted as loud as I could: *"Help!"*

The sound of my voice echoed and died away ineffectually. I took a deep breath and tried again: *"Help!!"* As before, the only answer was the wind in the pines.

It was the third time that I mustered some new source of strength, fueled by desperation, from as deep inside of me as I could go. It was a cry from the gut, a shout straight from the belly, and it was so loud and anguished that I could feel it burn my throat as my vocal cords vibrated like rubber bands.

"HELP!!!"

Nothing. As with the two previous distress calls, this one was also swallowed up into the vastness. Like a rushing wind, a feeling of complete desolation swept over me. I was alone, not the selfish solitude I'd attained on speed, but in real time and space, with the chill of my own fading echoes underlining my isolation. It was a realization worse than anything I'd gone through in the past confusing days. Hunger pangs and dehydration were severe but tolerable. The cold could cut me to the bone, but hadn't yet touched my spirit. But that loneliness was like a knife to the heart, and I could feel myself trembling with the pain of it.

Then it happened. I closed my eyes again, as much to block out the unbroken vista in front of me as to try and contain my own unbearable desolation. For the first time in my life, I listened to the silence inside my mind, without trying to fill it with my own thoughts and schemes and obsessions. No voice came to me, neither God's nor my own. Instead, I saw written on the inside of my eyelids, as plainly as the lines written on this page, two words: on the left eyelid was *Help.* On the right eyelid, *yourself.*

My eyes snapped open. I was breathing heavily. Almost afraid of what I had seen, I slowly closed them again. Once more, there it was, plain and unmistakable: *Help yourself.*

* * *

I MUST HAVE repeated that personal mantra five hundred times in the next hour. It may seem like an odd response to the situation I was in. Helping myself had gotten me nowhere. I needed the help of God, a passing helicopter, or the ski patrol. It was clear that there was no rescue on the way. I doubted whether anyone, with the possible exception of my parents, even knew, much less cared, where I was. Shouting for help had gotten me nothing but a strained throat. But I think it was just what I needed to hear at that point. The true dimensions of my peril had been made crystal clear, and I was confronted with the prospect of losing my feet, which had carried me so far in my life and career. If it really was God who had written those words on my eyelids, it was because He understood who I was, what it would take to get through to me, and to get me through. He wasn't asking me to pray for divine intervention, for angels to swoop down and carry me away, or for a sudden heat wave to turn the heavenly thermostat up in the dead of winter. He knew that I defined myself in large part by my own spirit of independence and autonomy, and He used that character trait to motivate and spur me on.

"Help yourself, help yourself, help yourself," I kept saying as I picked up my socks again and tucked them underneath my shirt next to my skin in hopes that they would dry there. Still holding my feet, I rubbed them slowly and thoroughly, using my thumbs to push into the skin and stimulate deep blood flow. With a branch, I fanned them until they were completely dry and then rapidly rotated my ankles and kicked my legs to force more circulation. I did the best job I could cleaning any snow, dirt, and debris from my feet and inside my boots, and when my socks were at least a little drier, I took them out and cleaned them as well. At first I wasn't sure what the strange stiff little particles were that had gotten stuck to the weave. It took me a minute to realize that it was more loosened skin, which had also been frozen and peeled away. I tried not to think about the fact that, while my efforts at restoring the feeling in my feet had helped to some extent, they were still like two stones attached to my legs. I just kept chanting "Help yourself" as I put the socks back on as delicately as I could and dialed the laces of my boots as snugly and comfortably as possible.

I was ready to go, and according to my best guess I needed to head back down to the river and follow it farther along the valley until I could find a place to cross over the ridge that would be roughly parallel to Tamarack on the other side. I strapped on my board, once again taking care to treat my feet tenderly, and found a place to launch myself down the steep incline. As always, the rush of acceleration gave me a boost and I was back at the banks of the river within a few minutes. Moving one strategic step at a time, I made it to the water's edge, then drank as much as I could hold, filling my trusty baggie and emptying it several times. It was at that point that I stumbled across one of the few signs of human activity that I had seen since my ordeal began: half buried in the snow by the river was an empty Coors beer can. I examined it carefully, as if it were a relic from some lost civilization, and thought for a long time about how I could make the best use of my discovery. In the end, I managed to take off both the top and bottom of the can and flatten out its thin aluminum body. It seemed to me that what I needed most was a way to attract the attention of anyone who might be out looking for me. I would utilize the shiny metal as a reflector and, for good measure, tied the top and bottom of the can to my bindings so that they too could catch the sunlight. I also attached the metal to my jacket so that it clanged as I walked, to scare away animals.

With my new equipment in place, and without pausing to consider what lay before me, I struck out across the featureless fields of snow. Once again I found myself plowing through waist-high drifts, and it was at that point that I began to feel my first serious hunger pains. My stomach had been growling for a while now, of course, but this was something different. My body felt tight and my muscles, especially in my torso, began to ache. Although I had nothing to compare it to, it felt to me as if my metabolism had actually turned on itself and, with no nourishment, was trying to absorb my own flesh and blood. I was eating myself, and, while I tried to shake that image, it stayed with me, accentuating the uncomfortable feeling that I was losing muscle mass from the inside. Before I finally got off the mountain, I would, in fact, have dropped forty pounds.

When I say that I had nothing with which to compare that feeling, that's not exactly true. It took me a while to recognize what increasingly seemed like a familiar sensation, until I remembered that this was exactly how I felt when I was coming down from a long speed run. As with frostbite, the similarities were striking. After it burns up all the energy that you've stored in your body, meth will move on to burn whatever else is available until all that is left is a flesh-draped skeleton. Adding to my discomfort was the persistent dehydration caused by the cold. Without replenishing liquid, my blood was getting thicker and my body had to work harder to circulate the blood.

Most of the rest of that third day since I had first ridden down Dragon's Back was spent in the deadening monotony of intense physical labor with scant measurable reward. The progress was minimal and there was no end in sight. To keep my mind off the enormity of what was facing me, I listened to the music on my MP3, carefully rationing my remaining battery life by turning it off after each rotation of the play list. Eventually I found myself focusing exclusively on Eminem's "Soldier." Something about its beat matched up with the rhythm of my own efforts, sticking one foot into the snow, pulling it out, setting it down and doing it all over again. If I ever have a chance to meet Marshall Mathers—aka Eminem—I'll be sure to thank him for a song that gave me consistent motivation and, more important, kept me company.

The heavy mist and fog would rise and fall depending

on the topography, alternating my visibility from ten to fifty feet and any distance in between. But generally it was impossible to see exactly where I was going or how much progress I had made. It wasn't until late that afternoon that I began to seriously second-guess myself, wondering if I was heading in the right direction after all and whether or not I would ever get to a place where I could cross the ridge and find Tamarack.

It was at that point that, like a mighty hand sweeping the clouds out of the sky, the view cleared for a brief minute and I could see for miles around me. It was miles of nothing, a faceless wilderness stretching in every direction, with my own tracks disappearing over a rise behind me. Trees, snow, ice, and rock blended into a blinding panorama just as the sun revealed itself above the mountain peak pointing to the station nine miles away at the top of Mammoth Mountain Resort. I was one ridge too far south. Now, it cast its long slanting rays against the ridge that separated me from Tamarack. The rock face soared over four thousand vertical feet, and I would have to fight my way up every inch if I wanted a chance to live.

CHAPTER NINE

Mom

EVEN THOUGH MY isolation felt absolute as night descended over my third day on the mountain, I also had reason for at least a glimmer of hope. By the next morning I was certain that it would become evident I was missing. I had a court date Tuesday for a hearing on the drug possession and trespassing charges I was facing after I'd fallen asleep in my car with a bag of meth in my lap. If I didn't show up, they would be issuing a warrant for my arrest. Of course, they'd have to find me first, and the irony of that struck me as I slowly began trudging up the sheer face of the ravine. I laughed: I was in a hiding place as big as all outdoors. What was the worst they could do to me? Swoop down and drag me off to jail? The thought of a nice warm cell and a peanut butter and jelly sandwich made me laugh again.

But the sound died in my throat when I realized that, by tomorrow morning, my parents would also know I was missing. The thought of the worry and anxiety my disappearance would cause them was no laughing matter. In fact, I had to choke back tears when I thought of the anguish I would be putting them through if I didn't get home soon. It was one thing for me to suffer the consequences of my own mistakes. But the last thing I wanted was for them to get caught up in this nightmare, too. They had given me so much, sacrificed everything to further my career and open the doors of opportunity. I simply couldn't bear the thought of causing them pain and was freshly motivated by the determination to return safely to them.

As my mom later told me, she knew almost immediately that something was wrong. "I'd gotten dental surgery the day before," she explained, "and when you didn't check in with me, I had an uneasy feeling. That wasn't like you. Even though I knew you were having problems, we've always had a strong bond, a connection that carried through no matter how far away you were. I tried to put it out of my mind, but there was a nagging feeling that wouldn't go away. I put in several calls to your cell phone, but it kept telling me that you were out of any service area. That just added to my concern. I finally called your father. He tried to reassure me, but it didn't do any good. Then, finally, when you didn't show up for your court date, my worst fears were confirmed. It was like you'd fallen off the face of the earth."

I might as well have. From the moment that the clouds

and fog had dispersed that afternoon, I saw the magnitude
of the climb in front of me. This was more than a Double
Black Diamond: it was the steepest, most difficult ascent
I'd ever seen. I had to fight back another wave of bleak despair. "What's the point?" a voice inside me said, and for a
moment, I couldn't come up with a good answer. Why not
just lie down in the snow and let the cold and exposure
take me away?

It was then that the image of my mother returned
again, vivid and alive in my mind. I'm not claiming that her
love and concern had somehow managed to bridge the
miles between us, but I do know that, at the point I
needed her most, she was somehow there. My mother is a
very strong woman, practical and down to earth, with a
no-nonsense edge in her New York accent. She never coddled or spoiled me, and when she laid down the law, it was
with the voice of clarity and authority. But I never
doubted for a moment that she loved me completely, and
that, regardless of the trouble I got myself in, she was always on my side. At the same time, I anguished over the
fact that I had kept so much of my life hidden from her. It
was as if I needed to maintain the ideal image she had of
me. I kept the reality of my drug addiction hidden, even
though there were times when I suspected that she knew
something was terribly wrong. I know she would have
done anything to help me if I could only have found a way
to let her know I was in trouble. I was in the most trouble

of my life now, and it was the remembrance of her steady, unwavering love that gave me the strength to go on.

By my best estimate, it was going to take two days to reach the top of the ridge that stood between Tamarack and me. That, all by itself, was a risky proposition. I was by no means sure I had the strength or stamina to survive two more nights in the wilderness, much less the endurance to make this perilous climb. If I reached the summit and discovered that I had once again miscalculated, it would be all over. I had made my best guess as to the direction of the lodge, but there was no way I could be certain of my calculations. I might be too far up or down on the ridgeback, the weather might close in, or I might simply be heading in the wrong direction entirely. I had to do what I could to maximize my chances.

Aware of the odds against me, I took out my MP3 player and switched it to the FM radio mode. Turning the dial, I locked onto the only signal available, a local Mammoth Mountain station with an adult pop play list. By pointing the MP3 at slightly different angles, I was able to get a bead on where the signal came in strongest. That was the direction I headed in. I had come up with a crude sort of compass and could only hope that it would lead me to safety by the most direct route.

It was already getting dark by the time I began to make my climb up the ridge. I hadn't gotten more than three hundred feet when it became evident that I needed to use whatever daylight was left to build shelter for the coming onslaught of night. But I was too exhausted to expend the necessary effort and too disoriented to focus fully on the task at hand. I sat in the snow, trying to catch my breath and gather my dwindling reserves of energy before it got too dark to see. But in the end I had waited too long. I was reduced to digging a trench in the side of the ridge, no more than two or three feet deep and just long enough to lie down in. By that time, night had fully fallen. It didn't matter. I just didn't have the strength to dig any deeper. There were no branches or limbs to raise myself up off the snow or to protect against the wind. I was exposed on the white face of nothingness.

And sure enough, I could hear its approach as it came whipping up the side of the ridge from across the valley like a runaway train. I propped my board at the lip of the trench, but the force of the wind knocked it down onto my head like a toy, as I struggled desperately in the darkness to lodge it again and block the blinding flurry of stinging snow. I huddled down in the trench, lying virtually unprotected on the naked side of the mountain, with nothing between the elements and me but that ineffectual windbreak.

I stayed like that for the rest of what was, by far, the most difficult night I had yet endured. The temperature dropped and the storm front swept back through with renewed fury, bringing with it another heavy fall of snow. The cold was beyond bone chilling. It was freezing my soul. My teeth chattered uncontrollably and my convulsive shivering only added to the encroaching sense of paralyzing exhaustion. I was too tired and too cold to move and instead curled up in a fetal position, reflexively clutching my crotch and waiting out the night. The sound of the howling wind haunted me, alternately a threatening roar and a mocking whine and occasionally breaking out into a full-throated shriek of primal rage. There were no wolves that night, no wild animals stalking me, but the wind was a far worse enemy, a powerful and malign assailant that was trying to tear me to pieces.

I lay there on the white face of nothing, waiting for daylight or death, whichever came first. When dawn finally broke, revealing a dull and overcast sky, I almost didn't realize it. Sometime in the long slow passage of the night, I had finally fallen asleep, oblivious now to the snow that fell even more fiercely. When I woke up, I was encrusted with an eight-inch blanket of fresh crystallized powder. I stood up, shaking myself free of the snow. I felt a hot surge of anger. I wasn't a frozen corpse quite yet. And I wasn't ready to lie down in my own grave, even if I had dug it myself.

THAT SENSE OF righteous indignation helped to spur my resolve to make real progress as my fourth day on the mountain began. I was going to go as far as I could as fast as I could and I swore to myself that I'd at least make it to the tree line on the ridge before another night fell.

"I will not be cold tonight," I muttered to myself, over and over.

It went without saying that the alternative would be to die trying. Of course, it wasn't easy to really gauge the task I had set for myself. The day had come up even cloudier and colder than previously, and there was no way I could actually see where the trees ended and the bare rock and snow began. As much as anything, it was a marker I had set in my own mind. It was the only method I had of measuring my progress.

But as the day wore on, I began to think about other ways that I could mark my ascent up the hill. It was important for me to know that I was actually advancing to my goal, that I could achieve what I'd set out to do by establishing what I'd already done. I decided I needed some milestones, so each time I stopped to rest, I would build a small snowman. The figures weren't much to look at, just random piles a few feet high with debris stuck onto them. But they gave me enormous comfort and encouragement. I was leaving some trace of myself and my journey behind, like a modern-day Hansel and Gretel. Maybe, I told myself, someone would find me by following them, like sentinels posted along the trail. I don't know if I really believed that or whether I was just fixated on establishing my existence in that trackless expanse, at least for a little while longer.

The day ended much as it had begun, with a grim and relentless march up that steep incline. As I had promised myself, I made it to the tree line, which was a good three quarters of the way to the top. With the onset of late afternoon shadows, I stopped by a large pine at the very edge of the bare face that opened up above me and began to make preparations for the evening's shelter.

As careless as my fatigue had made me the night before, I was now determined to do everything in my power to stay warm and protect myself from the infernal wind. I meticulously dug out a snow cave at the base of the tree and then systematically and savagely went about stripping off bark and branches from the nearby trees. When I had first gotten lost in the wild, I was careful about how I treated the foliage around me. I respected nature and didn't want to leave too much ecological damage behind, especially since I knew that taking bark off a tree might actually kill it. But by this time, such compunctions had long since been set aside. I attacked the majestic pines with all the strength I could muster, ripping down large swatches of bark and pulling off boughs and branches with abandon. I was determined to do anything I could to keep myself alive, and I knew only too well that I couldn't survive another night lying in the snow at the mercy of the wind. It was all about being as dry and warm as I could possibly make myself.

I dragged my makeshift insulation into the cave I had dug next to the tree trunk, and when I saw that it was still a skimpy shelter, I went back for more. I gathered enough to actually cover the walls and spread a thick layer on the ground beneath me. Finally arranging it to my satisfaction, I stepped back to take a look at my handiwork. I was proud of what I'd done; proud of the care I had taken to ensure my survival against the oncoming night.

Crouched at the mouth of my den, I pulled out my MP3 player to listen for any possible news that I might have been reported missing. After a few minutes of innocuous alternative rock, I turned it off and sat back to wait for darkness to fall.

As the dusky gray sky gradually grew dimmer, my attention turned to the climb I would be making in the morning. Past the tree line was nothing but the empty expanse of the ridge, and as I studied it my mind started to wander. There were some good runs here, it occurred to me, some sweet little cornices where I could pop off a hit or two and some elegant turns through the rocky outcroppings. The conditions were perfect, with a fresh fall of dry powder that, of course, was totally untouched. The reason I had come up here in the first place was to search for just such a riding paradise, and here it was, staring me in the face.

I got to my feet and grabbed my board. Ignoring my aching muscles, I climbed two hundred or so feet up the slope, strapped myself in, and launched out. It was like a reminder of another life I'd once lived, carefree and exhilarating, in tune with harmonious nature instead of locked in mortal combat with implacable and impersonal forces that showed no mercy. For those few brief moments, I forgot

NHL All-Star Game
with "The Great One"
Wayne Gretzky

Born to play

Eric with Mom and Dad at Long Beach

Clive Brunskill/ALLSPORT/Getty Images

Norway vs. Team USA; played to a 4–4 tie. 1994 Olympics at Lillehammer

Davis Barber Productions

Eric's intensity on the ice

Eric tripped up by his childhood friend
Robert Mendel, Northern Michigan
University vs. University of Wisconsin game

Rookie year face-off against former teammate Dean Antos

Rookie hockey card

(Top) National Guard Black Hawk helicopter rescue; *(Bottom)* The "animal"
Eric became after eight days on the mountain; *(Opposite)* Worried about his
feet, and wishing this blanket was soft cotton rather than wool

Frostbitten

Steep and deep, the perfect conditions Eric was always looking for

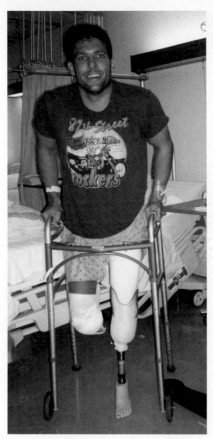

First time back on ice,
the Pickwick Ice Arena

Dangling

First time up at the
Grossman Burn Center

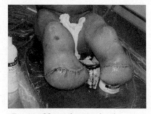

Cut off and stapled

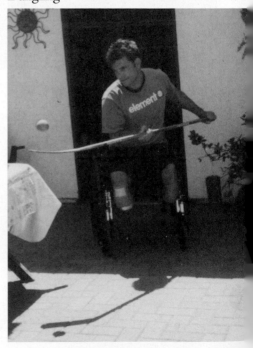

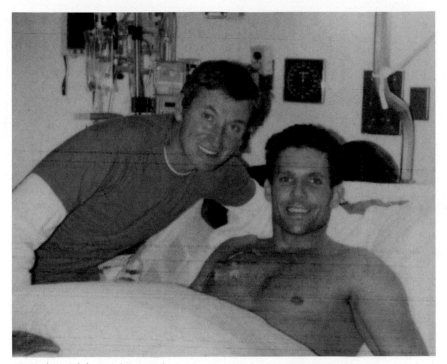

Gretzky visiting at hospital

Los Angeles County Jail card

Los Angeles County Jail
LEMARQUE
ERIC
8953712

Back on the board

Eric, Hope,
Nicholas,
Zachariah, and
Cherry-Snowball
Le Marque

Wedding day

Nicholas on ice

Eric with his
infant son, Zach

about everything, whisking through a frozen wonderland, letting the board take me where it wanted. I angled into a stop at the foot of the tree where I'd made my cave and, building another strong-walled-barrier after catching my breath, went up and did it again.

By now it was nearly dark and there was nothing left to do but climb into my sanctuary and settle in for the night. I had come to dread these interludes, the long minutes that dragged into long hours without anything to divert me but my thoughts and fears. I occupied myself with a pile of extra branches and bark I had set aside, stuffing them inside my clothes. It was uncomfortable and irritated the rash I'd been suffering from, but at least it provided a little more defense against the encroaching cold. To complete my snow palace, I tied my jacket sleeves to the bindings of my board and pulled it down like a trap door.

Nothing, however, could defend me from the hunger that suddenly and unexpectedly overpowered me in the gloom of that cave. After fantasizing for a while about what I'd eat when I got back—everything from a cheeseburger and fries to fresh grilled salmon and Caesar salad—I began experimenting with the pine needles and bark that lay around me. I discovered that I could choke down the seeds that I found still in their powdery pods and even scraped some of the soft inner tree bark off with my teeth. I remembered from my college ecology class that a deer's diet consists mostly of cedar leaves, but what I was chewing was simply too bitter to tolerate. My mind turned over the various possibilities of setting a trap for some small animal, a rabbit or a squirrel, using my frozen flesh as bait. Gruesomely, I even considered eating it myself. I wasn't thinking clearly enough to realize that those particular creatures weren't carnivores, but it was when I remembered the wolves that I set aside my delusions of being a great white hunter.

Eventually, like a dog chasing its tail, my thoughts circled back to my own helpless condition. I hadn't had the courage to take another look at my feet since that morning on the ledge, but I knew, even though they were completely numb, that water must have leaked into my boots again after the hard day I had spent slogging through the snow. I needed to do something to try and reverse the process that, in all likelihood, had already advanced too far to stop, so I unbound my boots and took off my socks. Sure enough, they were dripping wet. Wringing them out, I tucked them under my shirt again to dry against my skin. I pulled my feet as far up into my pants as possible and gathered more boughs and leaves to cover them up as best I could. I tried to ignore the needling and poking of the debris irritating my open wounds.

But there was nothing I could do when my restless mind once again turned to my parents. I suspected that by now they would know something was terribly wrong. I had always made a point of staying in touch with them, and now days had gone by without any contact at all. My heart ached to think what they might be going through, and tears welled in my eyes. I wept unashamedly, yearning to be delivered from the hell I was going through, as much for their sake as for mine.

"I knew you were in danger," my mother would tell me later. "It was something I could sense, as clear as day. But, at the same time, I was certain that you weren't dead. All I could do was pray that, wherever you were, God was watching over you, and that He would bring you back to me."

"Mom, Dad," I cried in the darkness, "if you can hear me, I'm all right. I'm coming home. I promise!"

Ten Steps

I DRIED MY tears. The last thing I needed was to get any more dehydrated. I comforted myself with the promise that, when I got back home, I would give my parents a reason to be proud of me. I had put them through a lot, not least the torment of seeing me spiral down into drug addiction. I wanted to make it up to them.

I wouldn't say I made a bargain with God, one of those deals you strike when you're in deep trouble and swear you'll be good if He pulls you out just this once. It was more than that. Ever since I'd spilled the last of my meth out into the river, I had felt a deep change in my outlook toward the drift my life had taken. It may seem strange, considering the dire circumstances I was in, but I had the certainty that I'd been brought to a new beginning, given a second chance to make things right. God had already granted me a reprieve from the slow, self-destructive death sentence to which I had condemned myself. It was now up to me to make good on the forgiveness I'd been granted. I would start by restoring the relationships I'd broken with the ones I loved, and who loved me, the most.

At least it gave me solace to make that pledge to myself, as I huddled in my dark cave, fragrant with the scent of fresh-cut pine branches. I closed my eyes. I didn't know how to pray, not exactly, but I felt a stirring of gratitude nonetheless. I was going to make it out of here, and when I did, it would be for a good reason. I had a new purpose in my life. I just had to live long enough to fulfill it.

Behind the darkness of my eyelids, I felt my chin slowly sinking down to my chest. The next thing I knew, bright morning light was streaming in through a crack in the entrance of my burrow. I had fallen asleep immediately and, for the next ten hours, plunged into a deep and dreamless rest. My exhaustion had finally overtaken me and it hadn't mattered whether I was cold or hungry and thirsty or still hypervigilantly on the alert for a roaming wolf pack. Sleep washed it all away and it felt amazingly good to realize that a long night had passed without me having to suffer through every hour.

I crawled out of the hole into the bright sunshine. The storm had finally passed and the sky was a cloudless blue spread out over the magnificent expanse of Sierra Nevada scenery. It was still cold, of course, but the padding of leaves and branches I had packed into my clothes had actually helped me to retain some body heat. The fact that it had come at the expense of an increasingly painful rash, aggravated by the sharp needles and the sticky tree sap, didn't bother me. The sky was bright, I felt well rested, and I was still alive: I had reasons to be thankful.

Opening my shirt, I pulled out my socks from where I had put them up against my skin. They had dried over the course of the night—another reason for gratitude. I slipped them back on my feet, trying not to focus on the dark purplish, almost black, color that had crept up from the flesh of my soles toward my ankles. I was just happy they were dry and was determined not to focus on anything negative on this new morning. "Help yourself," I said again. My feet still needed to take me out of there. Maybe there was still a chance I could save them, if I could only make it up the last ascent to the top of the ridge and, from there, down to the lodge. That was my task for the day and that was all I allowed myself to think about.

I pulled together my gear, making intricate adjustments to the fit of my goggles and gloves before I set out. My first steps were sure and confident, even if I was thrust once again into thigh-high snowdrifts. But I hadn't gone more than a hundred feet before I was dragged down by the gravitational force of my own depleted resources. It was as if, instead of having gotten a good night's rest, I hadn't slept at all. My reserves of energy were so drained that I could hardly keep my eyes open. My body was at last rebelling against the strain I had put it under for so long. Sleep, for me, had not brought rejuvenation, but rather the overpowering need for more sleep. I sat down to rest and immediately passed out, waking only when the sun had risen high enough to shine directly in my eyes.

Almost blinded, not by the glare from the snow, but from a pounding headache brought on by hunger and increasing altitude sickness, I struggled back onto my feet. I had to talk myself down from a panicked response to slowly starving to death. The sensation of my body metabolizing itself had been magnified over the past few hours, and it didn't do me much good to remind myself that, when I'd been on a meth run, I sometimes wouldn't eat for days. But this was different. Back then, it had been my choice not to touch food. Now that choice was taken away.

The intensity of my thirst was also expanding exponentially. The snow I had put in my baggie, and the rate at which it melted, was not nearly enough to relieve my dehydration, and in my weakened and confused state, I heard what I was convinced was the sound of water rushing under my feet. It all likelihood, it was the delirious memory of those figure-eight snow bridges over the river runoff that was causing the aural hallucination. But to me, it was both real and tantalizingly close. I began digging frantically to find the source of the flow until I was once again too worn out to stay awake and collapsed into the hole I had dug.

There was no way to tell how long I was out this time, but when I woke, dazed and blinking, the sun had moved higher across the sky and the first shadows of early afternoon had appeared over the landscape. A fresh wave of panic rose and I staggered to my feet and began thrashing through the steep drifts, frantic to get some distance, any distance, up the ridge. But after only a few more steps I was again struck with exhaustion like a hammer blow that virtually dropped me, face-first into the snow. I barely had the strength to turn around and, turning to the sun, I struggled to stay awake.

The rest of the day continued in the blurry and unreal realm between sleeping and waking. When I was able to stagger to my feet, I told myself that I had to take at least ten steps before stopping to rest again. Sometimes I made it, sometimes I didn't. Along with the burden of dragging my own wasted body through the wilderness, I felt as if I were carrying the weight of all the disappointment that had accumulated over the past several days. Every morning, I had told myself, would be my last on that mountain, and every night I had to face the same freezing purgatory. The frustrations and setbacks were starting to pile up, and since I didn't have anyone else to blame, I blamed myself. I felt disgraced. After hours of hopeless struggle, I could still see the shelter where I had slept the night before. The sight of it ate away at my hope.

THERE WAS NO use continuing. I needed, once again, to prepare for the onset of night. But my ability to plan and execute adequate shelter was a far cry from what it had been one night earlier when I carefully lined my snow cave with bark and branches. I just didn't have it in me and now, even a few hundred feet above the tree line, there was scant material available to do the job. I half stumbled, half crawled to the tall stump of a huge old pine tree that had somehow taken root in the thin air and soil before being battered down by the wind and weather of that rarified atmosphere. I dug out a shallow hole at the base and hunkered down in the well of the tree. There was nothing between me and the iron-hard earth and frigid snow pack surrounding me. With the rapidly falling night my hope also began to fade. I wondered if I was going to survive to see another morning.

Last night I had been so proud of the elaborate shelter I had made and the care I took to protect myself. Yet here I was, a day later, crouched in a hole, dreading the sound of the approaching wind. *Is this the best you can do?* I asked myself contemptuously. I hadn't made it more than a few hundred feet and didn't have the stamina to adequately shield myself against the elements.

Still beating myself, I fell into a heavy sleep, only to be awoken a few hours later by a sharp ache of thirst that felt like a fever peaking in my blood. Wanting water that badly was more than the simple desire to slake a need. It was like deprivation on a cellular level, as if every part of my being was screaming for relief. I was being denied the essence of life, my vitality slowly draining away as my body seemed to condense into itself. It didn't matter that I had been able to drink at least a little water from the melting snow in my baggie. When my thirst woke me up, I felt like I could swallow a lake and still not satisfy my craving.

As I swam back into consciousness, I realized that I had an urgent need to urinate. I had stored the water in my system for as long as possible, but as I became progressively more dehydrated, I was unable to efficiently expel the toxins that were building up and would have normally been washed out. Now was the time. I sluggishly moved out of the ditch I'd dug, and as I unzipped my pants, the anticipation of relieving myself inexplicably made my mouth water. I knew then what I had to do. Liquid was liquid, even recycled liquid, and I don't think I could have tolerated the splashing sound of emptying my bladder without at the same time somehow relieving my raging thirst. I took out my baggie and, packing half of it with snow, filled the rest with urine. Without hesitating, I drank it. It was warm and the smell was overpowering. I almost gagged trying to get it down, but there was no question about it. It gave me a moment of deep relief.

I didn't admonish myself this time. There were no recriminations about how the once proud hockey hero had been reduced to drinking his own piss. Instead I silently acknowledged my own potent will to live. There was nothing I wouldn't do, no extreme measure I wouldn't take, to survive.

But fighting for my life would take me *only* so far. And I had no way of knowing if it would be far enough. As I settled back into my hole, the sour taste of my own waste still in my mouth, I began to consider what would happen the next morning. I could feel my cold fear even more acutely than the frigid wind that whipped around the tree trunk. Although I had made precious little progress the day before, the fact was I was almost at the top of the ridge. Barring a complete physical collapse, I would be able to reach my destination sometime tomorrow.

But then what? Suppose I got there and was actually able to look over the spine of the ridge that had been my goal for so long. What if Tamarack Lodge wasn't waiting for me on the other side? What if, instead, I was faced with another panorama of endless hills and valleys, countless more miles of fresh-fallen snow and the face of Mammoth Mountain staring down at me like some vengeful god?

That bleak prospect was more than I could deal with. I tried feebly to push the thought out of my mind and hang on to the optimism that had brought me this far, but it was no use. I kept seeing the vast emptiness spread out below me and could feel the grip of utter despair like a cold hand around my heart. Did I really want to know what was on the other side of that ridge? After everything I'd been through, could I really handle the disappointment of another valley and beyond that another ridge and beyond that...?

It was in that moment that I came to the crushing knowledge that, despite what I had suffered and regardless of the relentless optimism I had worked so hard to maintain, there was a good chance I was not going to make it out of there alive. I had never seriously considered that option, or if I had, I'd still possessed enough self-confidence to push it out of my mind. *Help yourself.* Those simple words had taken me so far. Now, for the first time, I wasn't sure whether they would take me all the way.

In and out of sleep through the rest of the night, I fought a losing battle with the hopelessness and desolation that threatened to overwhelm me. I had started to obsess on the possibility that I was now even more lost than when I had begun and that the lodge was off in some other direction, or no direction at all. A voice inside that grew louder and louder in the darkness told me I was going to die. The truth was, I think I was already dying. My body was shutting down and I no longer had the strength to overcome the sinister certainty that had invaded my mind. It was no use telling myself that everything was going to turn out all right, that by tomorrow night I would be relaxing, my feet warm and restored, with all the good food and drink and creature comforts I could desire. There was no use telling myself that I would soon be able to give my mother a hug and let her know that I was okay and that, from now on, things were going to be different, that I had learned my lesson and changed my life. There was no use pretending. My long journey was going to end on the top of that ridge. One way or the other.

CHAPTER ELEVEN

The Stalker

BY THE MORNING of my sixth day on the mountain, the sun
had once again vanished behind a thick layer of clouds and
a heavy, clinging fog. But even in the dull gray light of
dawn, I felt a renewed sense of hope for the day. I was so
close to the top. I was sure if I could just pull myself up
those last hundred feet, it would be, literally, all downhill
from there.

I started out with the same determination I had summoned up the day before, choosing to overlook the fact
that my whole body felt weaker and more fragile. There
was a certain unavoidable logic to my predicament: I had a
finite amount of strength and stamina left and a finite distance to cover. Whichever of the two I would arrive at first
would dictate whether I lived or died. There was no percentage in trying to husband my reserves. I had no reserves. It was either give it everything I had or just give it
up. It wasn't going to be possible to replenish myself along

the way. Whatever energy was left, whatever motivation and mental stimulus, was going to be required for this last push.

I hadn't gotten more than a few feet from where I had slept the night before when I heard a distant, barely audible drone cutting through the cold air. I stopped and held my breath, trying to listen through the silence for the source of the sound. It seemed to be coming from the west, and sure enough, a few minutes later I caught sight of a black speck in the sky, moving almost imperceptibly toward me. My best guess was that it was a small plane, and maybe, just maybe, it was looking for me.

Trying desperately to clear my head, I looked around for something I could use to attract the attention of this potential search-and-rescue mission. There was nothing in any direction but the same rocks and snow I'd been trudging through since I'd moved up above the tree line. I had no time to pull together stones to spell SOS or drag my board through the snow to write HELP or any of the other dramatic devices I'd seen in countless movies. Then, as the faint whine of the airplane's engine came closer, I remembered one more cinematic cliché, the one where the shipwrecked survivor flashes reflected light from a pocket mirror.

Of course, the tin can mirrors I had weren't shiny enough to bounce off the dreary light of the overcast day. But I did have my MP3 player, with a tiny, three-inch-square LED screen. Fully aware that I was down to my last precious minutes of battery life, I turned it on and pointed it in the direction of the approaching plane. It was a futile attempt to be seen. Obviously, the music player was too small, and the glow from its screen too dim, to be seen even a short distance away, never mind from the altitude of several hundred feet at which the aircraft was cruising. I continued shining my feeble beam until the plane made a turn over the mountain and disappeared into the clouds. The silence that followed the fading purr was absolute. To keep from falling into abject despondency, I tried to tell myself that the plane was a good omen. Maybe by now they knew I was missing. Maybe they were actually looking for me.

Reassuring myself as best I could, I continued the climb. By now I had to use all the strength in my arms to pull my legs out each time they sank down into the snow, grabbing my thighs and yanking them up as hard as I could to make the next step. It would have been exhausting labor for even someone in the best shape. For me, it was torture. The overpowering urge to sleep continued to torment me as I forced myself up the steep incline. It took as much willpower to stay awake as it did to push through the snowdrifts, and within an hour it became clear that I was fighting a losing battle. What made it worse was that I knew what was happening to me. The physiological process was only too evident. As I continued to suffer from hypothermia, my body's need to preserve its remaining strength just to keep functioning was steadily becoming

more urgent. Instead of exerting myself to my last ounce
of strength, all I really wanted to do was to curl up in a ball
and sleep. Of course, if I were to succumb to that desperate necessity, the chances were I would never wake up. I
had to keep going, even if doing so was only prolonging
the inevitable reckoning of mortal flesh and blood against
merciless snow and rock.

Curiously, however, as the process of physical disinte-
gration inexorably wore on, my sensory capabilities became enormously heightened. I first noticed the change
when I began to smell a distinctly funky odor. It took me a
minute to realize that it was coming from me. After almost a week in the wilderness, I had really begun to stink,
but instead of just detecting the overall scent of an un-
washed body, I could actually distinguish the component
parts of my pungent smell. There was sweat, of course, but
my greasy hair also had a very distinct aroma, and I could
differentiate the sharp tang of the pine branches that I
had been sleeping on, mixing with my own reek.

But it didn't stop there. Driven by my thirst, I could
actually detect the delicate fragrance of the water locked
up in the frozen snow crystals. The same seemed to be
true of the minerals that comprised the rocks and stones
around me. My eyesight also became very acute. When I
peered into the fog, trying to see how far I had come and
how far I had to go, it was as if my eyes had developed an
uncanny telescopic ability. I would notice some small, almost indistinguishable feature in the landscape, and, al-

most as if a lens inside my mind had been activated, I could zoom in for a close-up. The effect was so startling that I imagined I could actually hear the click of the optical mechanism, like the mesh of tiny gears that was allowing me to view objects close up.

My hearing was likewise enhanced. I was able to deconstruct the myriad sounds that made up the seeming silence around me, from the distant flapping of bird wings to the slightest breeze blowing snowflakes across the rocks like the chiming of a thousand tiny bells. Nothing escaped my notice, but at the same time, I had no interest in utilizing my sharpened senses for anything other than as a potential tool for survival. If I saw or heard or smelled something that I thought might even remotely be helpful to me, I drew down on it like a laser beam. As I struggled through the snow, I would stop every time I walked across a branch or tree limb that had been buried in the snow, even this far above the tree line. I pulled it out to examine it carefully and, after collecting a handful of broken boughs, puzzled over how I might weave them together, using the straps on the bindings of my board to create an improvised pair of snowshoes. I even went as far as searching for small stones with sharp edges to use in unscrewing the binding in order to loosen the straps. I also tried using the condo key and some of the tin can. Everything I thought, everything I did, and everything I experienced was channeled through the filter of my struggle for survival.

It was well into the late afternoon when I at last arrived at the final approach to the top of the ridge. I hadn't climbed all that far, yet it had drained every last bit of my energy and determination. I was completely spent, but that doesn't really explain what I did next, or why. The reality was, I still had enough daylight left to make it to the ridgeback and look over the other side. But as I got closer, I started to hang back. The fear of not finding what I had staked my life on was more than I could face, especially in my weakened and depleted condition. I told myself that it made more sense to spend the night close to the summit where I could gather what was left of my strength for the descent the next morning. But I was deluding myself. The reality was, I really didn't want to know what was on the other side of that ridge. The prospect of peering down to nothingness was too terrifying, like looking to an abyss that looks back at you. I was willing to endure another freezing night rather than to confront my own worst fear.

It may seem strange to imagine that, faced with the possibility of knowing my fate, I chose not to know. But I had been through so much. Meth, wolves, waterfalls, and hallucinatory dreams. Thirst, hunger, and cold. Loneliness and isolation and the terrible knowledge that the ones I loved were suffering on my account. If, after all of that, I discovered that there was still no escape from the frozen hell around me, wouldn't it be easier just to finish it off then and there? Perhaps tomorrow, if I lived that long, I would find the courage to gaze over the top of that ridge.

But right then, I couldn't summon the nerve. It was beyond me, almost as if I was afraid to leave the wilderness to face the unknown.

SUFFICE IT TO say, there would be no elaborate campsite that night. I could hardly scrape away enough snow to make a shallow trench for myself, although by the time darkness fell I had managed to hollow out enough of a cave to be shielded from the wind. I crawled into my lair like a wounded animal and, closing my eyes, instantly fell asleep.

I woke up just as quickly a few hours later, startled by a surge of dread that had roused me from a deep sleep. I had heard a sound, something just beyond the black night. I was sure of it. The wolves had come back, I told myself, grabbing the dagger that I had carved from a scorched branch and carried with me ever since. I could feel their eyes on me, unblinking and patient, waiting for me to fall asleep again before they tore into me in a fury of fangs and snarling jaws.

Sitting bolt upright, I brandished my crude weapon, yelling and screaming as I had done that first night, so long ago, in the valley of the shadow of death. This time, however, my cry was a hoarse and feeble croak, sounding in my ears less like a warning to stay away than an invitation to move in for the kill. The uncanny certainty that I was being watched had only grown more urgent. I was convinced that the enemy, some nameless and lethal foe, was lurking close by and that I had to stay vigilant and alert to ward it off. I propped up my faithful board at the entrance to the cave and crouched down, clutching my knife, ready for the inescapable fight.

I don't know when I woke up again. It was still pitch black and the knife was still in my hand. The only thing that had changed was the shuddering presence of that invisible adversary, much closer now, but still watching and waiting. I tried to scream again, to scare it away, but my throat constricted around the fear that rose from my belly. I was helpless in the face of this presence, so menacing and malevolent. In my delirium, I also felt something hauntingly familiar, as if the creature had been pursuing me the whole time I had been on the mountain. It was then that I understood how it had actually been following my trail for even longer than that, and what flashed through my mind was the rush of meth, which had always brought me such ecstatic bliss. Every time I'd gotten high, I now realized, this specter had approached one step closer. I was being stalked by death. I had been for a long time and I could hear its breath in the rustle of the wind, see its dark shape against the halogen glow of the snow, and feel its eyes every time I closed my own.

People talk about near-death experiences. Sometimes it's a white light. Sometimes it's your life flashing in front of you. But it wasn't like that for me. Instead, it was as if a familiar stranger had stepped from the shadows to make himself known, somebody very real who also knew me all too well. I had courted death with reckless disregard for my life. Now, in the dead of night, in a snowy hole on a remote mountaintop, the summons had been answered. Death was coming for me.

That's how it felt anyway. In reality, it had to have been a combination of hypothermia, dehydration, starvation, pure exhaustion, and the last lingering effects of the speed that was being leeched from my body. But whatever it was, it felt more like reality than anything I'd ever experienced. There was nothing outside my cave, of course, no track or trace of a visitor in the night. It was all happening inside my fevered brain; a hallucination, a nightmare, a vision. But when dawn finally broke, I didn't need prints in the snow to prove that I had had an encounter with extinction. The evidence was in the chill that had reached down through my skin and bones to touch my soul.

As I was grappling with this demon of my own devising, my parents meanwhile had decided to take matters into their own hands. "We couldn't just sit around and wait anymore," my mother recounts. "We called the police, but we weren't willing to just stand by while they conducted a search. We both had a sense that time was running out, so we did a little investigating on our own. After talking to a few of your friends, we got the address of where you were staying in Mammoth. Your father and his girlfriend, Stella, volunteered to drive up there and see if they could track you down.

"Those were some of the most anxious hours of my life. I kept telling myself that, when they arrived, they'd find you safe and sound. I was ready to be both relieved that you were okay and angry that you had put us through so much. But in my heart, I knew it wasn't going to happen that way. It was just not like you to be out of touch for so long. Something was wrong and I had the feeling that soon enough they'd find out what it was. It was almost better not to know. I kept praying for the best outcome, even as I tried to prepare myself for the worst."

My dad and Stella pulled up to the condo I had borrowed late on the sixth night of my ordeal, even as I was fighting my pitched battle with death. They had gotten a key from the owner and made a quick search of the place. "It broke their hearts to see clothing and equipment that they knew belonged to you," my mother told me. "But they had to focus on the task at hand. They took a quick inventory of everything and realized that what was missing was your snowboard. It was obvious to both of them then where you were and the danger you were in. Your father immediately made a call to the ski patrol, and went to the police station early the next morning."

Once again, however, they weren't satisfied with just reporting my disappearance to the authorities. "They 'd brought up a picture of you," my mother continued. "They went to a print shop and had a bunch of copies made and then took the gondola up to the ski lifts. They handed out the pictures to every snowboarder they could find, asking them if they'd seen you and to keep an eye out for you. They were there most of the day, hoping against hope that one of them would come back with some news. By the afternoon, when they 'd heard nothing and the ski patrol had come up empty-handed, I think they both began to fear the worst. But we never gave up hope. We believed that you were alive and that belief was like a lifeline that I kept throwing out to you."

My mother's words, like the strange and supernatural brush with death I had on the mountain, became, for me, the evidence of things not seen. That's how the Bible describes it: the unseen world that reaches into our reality. Maybe in times of crisis, or extreme danger or the terrible jeopardy of a loved one, that world comes a little closer. We see things more clearly; we understand just how fragile we are and how much we depend on grace and mercy to sustain us. I accept the reality that death came near to me that night. I acknowledge that it was my mother's prayers that kept me alive. I can't explain it. I don't have to. It's enough that I know it's true and that I'm alive today to testify to that truth.

CHAPTER TWELVE

Reset

I WAS TEN steps from the top of the ridgeback when I woke the morning after my spooky encounter with the grim reaper. I could clearly see my destination out the mouth of my cave. But it might as well have been twenty miles. I had nothing left to carry me to the top. It was over. I was finished. Fear still had something to do with my paralyzed condition, the awful uncertainty that maybe I had traveled one valley too far to the south or that Tamarack may not lay over the ridge that had taken me four days to climb. Yet even if I had somehow been able to summon the resolve to find out whether I was right or wrong, I had lost the physical ability to even climb out of my hole and find out the truth.

I had been lost for seven days now, a solid week without food or shelter, hiking through deep snow in freezing temperatures and driven to the point of insanity by loneliness and exposure. Through it all, I clung to the conviction that I would make it back alive. But when the moment came, I fell short. My fear of death was tangible. I had felt it hovering close to me. But fear wasn't enough to pull me through. The love I had for my parents was powerful. I wanted more than anything to survive for their sake. But love wasn't enough to get me over that hump. The pride I had in my own abilities and resourcefulness was strong. I had come this far by learning how to stay alive in the most hostile of environments. But my self-confidence couldn't pick me up and carry me home. I had reached the end of myself. I didn't know what lay beyond. For the first time in my life, I was truly and completely helpless.

For the rest of that day, I never left the shelter I had dug. The sun rose, clouds rolled overhead, and the hours unwound as morning turned to midday and moved steadily on into the afternoon. It all passed me by. I may not have been dead yet, but it was hard to tell the difference. I had passed into a state of sleep so heavy and profound that nothing—not cold, not hunger, not thirst—could wake me. If I stirred during that long silent interlude, I don't remember it. If I had dreams, they drifted by unseen. If I realized that where I lay might well become my grave, I didn't care. For all I knew, I was already petrified, my blood frozen and my flesh turned to stone. There was no difference now between me and the environment against which I had fought so long and hard. The mountain had prevailed and I had become a part of it.

The deep slumbering spell I was under lasted until twilight and then on through the night. I would have been an easy picking for any predator that had sniffed me out, and in my vulnerable condition the cold could have certainly finished me off. But that didn't happen. Instead the spark of life kept flickering deep inside, my heart kept beating and my blood, however sluggishly, kept pumping. I was saving myself by sleeping, maintaining the minimal physical functions required to sustain respiration and circulation. And at that point, consciousness was a luxury I couldn't afford.

The night deepened, passing into the predawn hours before the eastern sky began to lighten at last. It was only then that, like a patient coming out from under anesthesia, I finally started to swim up through the thick layers of sleep that had buried me. I had been lying motionless in my hole for thirty-six hours. It was the morning of my eighth day on the mountain.

Of course, I had no way of knowing how much time had passed. It was only later that I was able to make any sense of those last, lost days. But I suspected I had been sleeping for a long time by how stiff and aching my muscles were. It was as if rigor mortis was already beginning to set in.

There is a phenomenon that often occurs with dying people in which they briefly become very lucid. It's as if their life reasserts itself in one last burst of energy and they come back into themselves temporarily before slipping away completely. I think something like that happened to me that morning. Still half-asleep, I was somehow totally aware of myself and my surroundings. I took a slow inventory of my body parts. My feet were still completely numb, but the rest of me seemed to be present and accounted for. I checked to see if my meager gear was in place, and sure enough, my board was still perched at the lip of the cave where I had propped it. The smell of urine clung to my baggie, but it had become a treasured possession and I carefully filled it one more time with snow. Then I carefully took out my MP3. The battery indicator had shrunk to a single bar for as long as I could remember, and when I turned it on I saw that it had begun blinking a warning that I was nearly out of juice.

Then, suddenly, an idea occurred to me, an inspiration that came directly from my strangely heightened state. The FM tuner would only bring in one signal, the easy-listening station from Mammoth. But what if I were to tune the device slightly off that broadcast frequency? If the player kept trying to bring in that station, could it possibly be sending a beam that could be picked up by anyone who might be out searching for me? It was worth a try. As I said, I was thinking with extraordinary clarity that morning, as if a dense fog had lifted just before the onset of total darkness.

I began trying to adjust the MP3 to see if I could get close to the station without tuning it in completely. That's when I heard it. Someone said my name! My fingers trembled almost uncontrollably as I turned up the volume and prayed that the battery wouldn't give out.

It was a local news program. "The Mammoth Mountain ski patrol has been searching for a snowboarder by the name of Eric Le Marque," the announcer reported. "After initially uncovering evidence of a cave shelter in a remote area on the eastern face of the mountain, the patrol has been able to locate signs of Le Marque but was unable to continue due to the treacherous conditions. Since it has been over a week since he disappeared, the snowboarder is presumed dead and the authorities have announced that they are asking the National Guard to send a helicopter to assist in a body recovery operation."

Suddenly the sense of utter isolation that had been my constant companion from the beginning of my ordeal had vanished, leaving behind a giddy, almost dizzying joy. I wasn't alone after all. I had a name, an identity that connected me back to a world I thought I would never see again. There were other people, out looking for me at that very moment. I wasn't the last man on earth and there was more to my existence than trudging toward that huge, empty horizon of snow.

I was panting with excitement now, but my happiness was quickly replaced by a sharp resentment. A body recovery operation? "I'm not dead yet," I proclaimed out loud. "Eric Le Marque is still alive, dude." It felt good to say my name, to hear the syllables spoken, not just on the radio, but in my own audible voice. For days now, I had felt like a phantom, hovering between life and death. Now, all at once, I was back in my body, and I could feel the surge of energy that came with it. I was angry at being given up for dead, and that anger was all the incentive I needed to keep on living.

ALL I HAD to do now was to survive long enough to get found. There was no stopping me now. I would be saved today. It was over. I gathered up my things, the pathetic collection of odds and ends that had served me so well, and, after a full day and a half, finally emerged from my burrow. As I stood up, trying to maintain my balance after lying prone for so long, the mental acuity I had awakened with suddenly dissolved. I felt dizzy and light-headed. The day had come up cloudy, but the light reflecting off the snow hurt my eyes and I saw black spots swimming in my field of vision. What had previously been a sensation of clearheaded consciousness had now become a muddled and cluttered confusion of thoughts and feelings. I knew I had some reason to be happy and hopeful, but I had trouble remembering what it was. Was I going to be rescued? Was I going to die? I wasn't sure which was which and I began to wander aimlessly around in circles, as if trying to find the missing clue to the mystery of these final hours.

After taking a few steps, I fell flat on my face. My frostbitten feet had lost their resiliency and the ability to flex with my steps. I was walking on flat frozen feet and it

was almost impossible to stay upright. I staggered to my
knees, took another step, then fell again, lying in the snow
and trying to figure out what was happening to me. The
mountain scenery was tilting at a crazy angle, the sky was
sideways, and I could feel my body twitching like something in its death throes.

It took me a long time, maybe an hour, maybe more, to
get myself back together and take stock of what was happening to me. My head had cleared a little and my first
thought was for my feet. I glanced down at them and what
I saw seemed to register from a long way off, as if I were
looking through the wrong end of a telescope. One foot
was frozen in its boot, unlaced, with no sock. The other
was bare. Somewhere along the way I had lost my other
boot. I had to find it, I told myself, but then forgot what I
was looking for. When I remembered again, the day had
moved along like the hands of a speeded-up clock.
Shuddering with the realization that more lost hours had
passed, I reached down to my remaining boot, still a long
way off, and began turning the lacing dial. I rotated it manically, cinching it up tighter and tighter until it gave way
and the laces went slack. It broke, but I continued futilely
turning it as I tried to process what had just happened.
The question of how to fix the broken rotor took on
cosmic significance as I sat in the snow and mulled over
the possibilities in my mind. My mental abilities were
shutting down, one function at a time. Time was an elastic
concept, stretching and contracting according to rules I

didn't understand. Logical deductions became complex riddles that were both fascinating and frustrating to my befuddled brain. Even my own sense of impending death felt unreal, as if it were happening to someone else on another plane of existence.

As I stared dumbly at the snapped laces in my hands, I entered a half-waking, half-dreaming state in which I was convinced that I was actually in the middle of a complex and challenging video game. The aim was to get to the next level, which was either death or deliverance, I wasn't sure which. I needed to concentrate and focus to overcome the obstacles that kept me from the next phase of play, but I kept slipping back, doing the same things over and over without understanding why. I looked around me in the snow, searching for a reset button. It had to be around here somewhere. If I could just find it, I could start again, get the hang of playing and finally beat the game.

At that point, my hyper-attuned senses kicked back in, but in a wholly different way. Suddenly I was outside of myself, watching impassively as I brushed aside snow looking for the imaginary reset button. I could see myself in every detail: the long greasy hanks of hair, the scraggly growth of week-old beard, the tattered and torn clothing. The stink now was overpowering and the raspy breath I drew from the cold air sounded like a dull saw cutting through rotted wood. I was pathetic, but this time I wasn't ashamed or disgusted by what I had become. I felt a kind of gentle sorrow, a tenderness for my mortal flesh that was perishing by slow degrees. I can't say I had one of those genuine out-of-body experiences that they talk about. In some ways I was still playing my imaginary video game, once removed from reality. But I knew beyond any doubt that if I didn't make it off this mountain today, I never would. This is where I would die, and as the realization came to me, it was accompanied by a deep feeling of serenity and surrender. I was fading away and soon I would be gone, leaving behind all the suffering I had endured. I felt bad for my parents, but for myself I had only compassion. One way or the other I would soon be at peace.

Then, as quickly as I had drifted off, I was back, inside my own head, once again occupying my wracked and trembling body, *You're dying,* I told myself, and in that instant I snapped out of it. The peace and tranquility were gone. So were the fear and doubt. What replaced them was a fierce determination. It wasn't my time. I had been born into this world for a purpose, and that purpose had yet to be fulfilled. Maybe I would die today, but I would die trying to stay alive, even if it meant crawling over the top of that mountain on my hands and knees.

I slapped myself harder and harder. I wanted to be reminded that I still had feeling and that being able to feel meant that I was still alive. The slap hardly registered, so I did it again, harder this time. When that didn't work, I balled up my fist and punched myself. That got to me. I could feel the pain in my jaw. I hit myself a second time and then a third. It felt good. It felt real. This was no video game. What was happening was actually happening. Life was all around me, even on the desolate extremes of that barren ridgeback. I didn't want to leave it behind. I had too much left to do. I socked myself once more for good measure. *You're alive,* I said to myself. *Don't you forget it.*

That's when I heard the helicopter.

CHAPTER THIRTEEN

Black Hawk

MY LAST DESPERATE gambit had worked. The MP3 player, trying to pull in a clear radio broadcast, had transmitted just enough of a signal for the National Guard Black Hawk chopper to pick up a faint trace on the back side of the mountain. With a general area to search in, they had utilized their infrared heat-seeking equipment and were able to zero in on me.

When I heard the familiar drone of the helicopter blades, I immediately got up and, standing as best as I could on my frozen feet, scanned the horizon for any sign of a rescue approach. Taking off my goggles, I was temporarily blinded by the burning glare of the sun on the snow. It was getting on toward midafternoon, a little after 2:30 p.m. I had spent the whole day within a few yards of my cave and was no closer to my ultimate goal, the top of the ridge, than I had been two days earlier.

The noise of the approaching aircraft got steadily

louder, and suddenly, like a sea creature breaching the waves, it reared up over the ridgeback, roaring in low over the ground and speeding past me. For one horrendous moment, my heart sank. I was sure that they had missed me, and I waved my arms frantically, my frozen shirt tearing at the scabs and open sores on my arms and torso. The chopper flew rapidly down the flank of the valley. But then, with a wide turn, it came back around and hovered over me at about twenty feet. The racket was deafening and the snow around me swirled up in furious funnels, whipping at my face. I squinted up at the belly of the chopper in time to see the side door open and a figure in a sleek silver suit descend on a rope, like some character out of a science fiction movie, or a vision of the stalker I had imagined the night before.

It was over. Whatever happened from here on out, I had survived. It was a profound relief to imagine my parents' smiling faces and to know that I wasn't going to bring them any more pain and grief. I had prevailed against enormous odds, but there was an oddly anticlimactic feel to this moment, as well. It seemed like I should be basking in the pride of my achievement, but I couldn't summon up the feeling. In time I would realize how close I had come to death and how much it had been a simple matter of timing and luck that I had escaped my fate. I hadn't prevailed. I'd been spared.

There was also a twinge of disappointment in the fact that, for all the effort I had expended, I hadn't actually made it to the top of the ridge. I was so close and now, with the chopper hovering overhead, I wanted more than anything to see if I had been right. Was Tamarack Lodge on the other side? Actually, what I wanted more than anything, I suddenly realized, was to ride my board down the slope, just as I had been imagining for so long. That was going to be my payoff for all the hard work it had taken me to get up there, and now, suddenly, I was going to be whisked off the mountain before I had a chance to charge some freshies on the way down. I would have been the only one ever to ride that section of the mountain.

The man in the foil suit, who I assumed was a Guardsman, made his way toward me on a pair of high-tech snowshoes.

"I could have used those," I said to him as he approached.

He laughed. "I'll bet," he replied. "You'd probably be up this mountain in no time." He took off his goggles and mask. "Are you Eric Le Marque?" he asked. I nodded. "Say it," he continued.

"Say what?" It was hard to hear him over the roar of the chopper hovering above us.

"Say your name," he told me.

"Eric," I replied, slightly puzzled. How many lost people was this guy looking for up here? "Eric Le Marque."

After he asked me a few more times, I realized that it was standard procedure in rescue operations. He needed to know what kind of mental and physical condition I was in, and knowing my name was a basic criterion. His next move was to stick a thermometer in my mouth.

He did a double take when he read my temperature. I later found out it was eighty-six degrees. "Okay," he said. "Here's what's going to happen. The chopper is going to circle back and hover at two hundred feet and drop a high-speed hoist. It's a two-man T-bar perch not unlike a ski lift seat. You'll get on," he continued. "I'll keep hold of you with one hand and put my other hand out so we don't spin on the way up. We'll take you home."

"Okay," I said. "Just let me get my stuff." My board was around somewhere and I still had to find that missing boot.

He shook his head, putting his goggles back on and taking me by the arm. "You don't need it," he said. "We've just got to get you out of here right now."

I looked at him like he was crazy. I wasn't about to leave my board behind. That would be like deserting my best friend, "Burton." It wasn't just the fact that the board had cost me nearly a thousand dollars. It was that it had literally saved my life on more than one occasion. I had used it to get into this predicament and had depended on it to get me out. Along the way, I had formed a powerful bond, an almost human connection between it and me.

"Look," I said. "I tell you what. Pick me up on the other side of the ridge and I'll just ride down to the bottom. It'll be easier that way."

Now it was his turn to shoot me a skeptical look.

"That's probably not a good idea," he answered in the soothing tone he might have used to talk to a child. "What do you say we just take you back?"

"No, really," I replied. "I can ride down. Then maybe you guys can drop me off where I'm staying. I'd really appreciate it."

He gently eased me over to the platform and then quickly sat down opposite me, gripped me around the shoulder, and signaled to the hoist operator. As we were pulled up, I spotted my board, stuck forlornly in the snow not far from the cave. I felt a sharp pang of remorse and a lump in my throat. *Maybe,* I thought distractedly, *I can come back later and pick it up.*

As we were pulled into the belly of the chopper, I was still struggling to comprehend what had just happened. For the first time in over a week, I was relating to other human beings, and while I felt tremendous gratitude toward the rescue crew, I also wanted to be by myself for a little while longer. I needed time to readjust and reenter the world. "Just take me somewhere where I can catch a bus back to the condo," I persisted to the rescuer. "I can find my way back from there."

"We should probably take you to the hospital," he said, in the same measured and even tone. "Just to get you checked out." He reached over to unzip my jacket. "You're a little wet," he continued. "You must be cold." He handed me a wool blanket, stiff and scratchy. I wrapped it around myself, but couldn't help wishing they had given me something a little softer and more comfortable. It didn't seem as if there was all that much difference between the blanket and the pine needle insulation I had provided for myself.

Another National Guardsman began taking pictures of me, and the sound of the automatically adjusting camera lens reminded me of the enhanced powers of perception that I had experienced on the mountain. I must have had a strange look in my eyes, because the guy in the silver suit leaned forward and shouted over the roar of the engine, "You doing okay, Eric?"

I nodded, but my attention was elsewhere. As the chopper peeled off back toward the east face of the mountain, we rose above the ridgeline. There, on the far side, I could see the Nordic ski track that leads to Tamarack Lodge. I had been right all along and that sudden knowledge overwhelmed me. Tears welled in my eyes as I turned to my rescuers.

"This is the first time I've ever been in a helicopter," I said.

THERE WAS BARELY time to enjoy the ride. The trip to Mammoth Hospital was over in a matter of moments, and when we landed at the chopper pad, there were emergency room staffers standing by with a gurney. I ignored it and began to climb out of the cargo bay to make my way across the concrete on my own. One of the nurses stopped me.

"No sir," he instructed. "Get on this and lie down."

It seemed completely unnecessary to me. I had walked for miles on my own and didn't need to be wheeled anywhere now. I'd been saved. All I wanted them to do was go through their procedures and let me be on my way. I needed to get back to the condo, have a good soak, something to eat, and maybe a nap. I was even considering trying to find some more equipment and get back up on the mountain. After all, I had already missed my court date. What was the reason for hurrying back now? There was still plenty of good powder up on the runs. Maybe I could get in a couple more days of riding.

I obviously wasn't thinking straight. Part of my delusion was the need to reclaim the life I'd left behind a little more than a week ago. I was unwilling to admit that the comfortable circumstances I'd been living in had changed forever. Another part of my delirium was simply that I didn't want to acknowledge what my real physical condition was. My feet had no feeling below the ankle. Maybe if I ignored that reality, it would go away.

But the hospital staff wasn't about to let me go anywhere. They put me on the gurney, but instead of lying down as I was instructed, I sat up as they pushed me through the hospital doors. It was my way of asserting my independence and the first step in what would become an ongoing struggle to maintain my own autonomy in the weeks and months to come.

I was taken immediately to an ER examination room, where a group of doctors stood just outside the door in an urgent, whispered conversation. I still had remnants of the superacute hearing and wanted to shout at them, "I can hear you! Why don't you come in and tell me to my face?" I didn't appreciate being left out of the loop. The least they could do was shut the door. But somehow I couldn't quite summon the energy to raise my voice and instead just glared at them as they would occasionally throw me a concerned look.

In the meantime, the nurses were quickly and efficiently going about their routine. I was immediately hooked up to an IV, and as soon as they determined that my foot was frozen into my boot, they brought a pan of hot water and poured it in to melt the ice. Meanwhile, another caregiver had begun to cut away my pants with a pair of scissors.

"Hey," I said, "you don't have to do that. I can get out of them myself." Once again I was thinking about both how much the pants had cost me and how they had protected me during my ordeal.

But no one paid any attention and they continued to strip my clothes off to get me ready for a thorough exam. When I was brought a cup of ice chips to suck on, I almost laughed out loud. I had seen nothing but frozen water for eight days and had done my best *not* to eat it to keep my body temperature from dropping. Was this the best they could offer?

"How about a hot toddy?" I asked no one in particular. "Or some hot chocolate?" I started salivating at the thought of a steaming mug topped with whipped cream. But I was quickly learning that I was now subject to procedures and protocols that had nothing to do with my own needs or desires. After spending all that time on the mountain surviving by my wits and instincts, it was frustrating to be maneuvered and manhandled by total strangers like a piece of meat.

They had finally gotten all my clothes off and wrapped me in a blanket, when my parents were escorted in. It was great to see them again, a reunion I had imagined many times on the mountain, but it wasn't exactly how I'd pictured it. Instead of the joyous laughter I had expected, their faces dropped as soon as they walked in the room. Though they tried to hide their shock and concern, it was only too obvious to me.

"You looked terrible," my mother would later tell me. "You had lost so much weight, it was like seeing a famine victim. And the skin on your face was blistered and raw. We thought for sure they would have to cut some of it away and you'd be permanently disfigured. Of course, we were so happy to see you alive, but it was very difficult to cope with the condition you were in."

By the same token, it was difficult for me to cope with the fear, almost horror, that they projected. Suddenly all my schemes of getting out of the hospital and returning to business as usual evaporated. Their expressions reflected the true state I had been reduced to. It was no use trying to reassure them, to pretend that everything was going to be all right. They could see the truth, and what they saw, I saw too, mirrored in their eyes.

At the same time, I felt terribly guilty. The major motivation that kept me going for all those days was to spare them the pain and suffering of my death. But this was almost worse. I couldn't shake the feeling that I had done something wrong. This was all my fault and there was nothing I could do to make it better.

"I'm sorry, Mom and Dad," I said in a choked whisper. Tears sprang to their eyes as they rushed over to embrace me. I gestured to my mother and she leaned in close. "Mom," I said, my voice barely audible. "Mom, don't look at my feet. Just don't look at my feet."

CHAPTER FOURTEEN

Popsicles

I HAD LIVED through a punishing test of mental and physical endurance. After eight days, I had endured longer than anyone else in the history of Mammoth. It was an impressive exploit, a testament to one man's sheer will to survive. But it paled in comparison to what I was about to go through.

In many ways I was equipped to handle what I had to face on the mountain. My life revolved around being fit and I was accustomed to meeting physical challenges head-on. On the other hand, of course, my addiction had left me woefully unprepared to make sound decisions that might have kept me out of harm's way to begin with. But once I was in that frozen hell, I could call on resources that I had developed over my entire life.

But there was no way I could have anticipated what I would have to confront after I was rescued. I didn't have the emotional or even mental maturity to really understand the toll I had taken on myself, or how to begin the healing process. My only response to the crisis I faced was to try to escape. Running away worked until it didn't work anymore, and by then, I had reached a bottom too deep to dig myself out of alone. I needed help, and it was when I finally realized that that the process of restoration really began.

But I had a long way to go to get to that place in those first few days being laid up in a hospital bed, with a view of Mammoth Mountain out my window. After the trauma of my ordeal and distress of seeing my parents so distraught, all I wanted was to shut my eyes and make the world go away. I did it the only way I knew how: through drugs.

Although I really wasn't suffering beyond a raging hunger, persistent thirst, and gashes, scratches, and rashes, I told the nurse that I was in acute pain and needed relief. It was a lie, but not a total lie. The visit from my parents had left me deeply depressed and anxious. In one moment of clarity, I had been able to admit to my mother what I couldn't admit to myself—that I was in danger of losing my feet to frostbite and infection. Once I had said it out loud, revealing to her the fear and sense of shame I felt, I wanted to forget all about it. It was a pattern that I would repeat over and over in the days to come, acknowledging reality only to flee in the other direction as fast as I could.

The nurse gave me a shot of painkiller, and as I sank into a drug-induced haze, I realized that I had been on a ragged edge, with my senses operating on overload, for eight days. Adrenaline had been pumping through my body at a constant rate, and my fight-or-flight instinct had been cranked to the max. Now, with the sedative spreading through my body, I was finally able to fully relax. As I got calmer, I was also able to let go of some of the sadness I was feeling. Perhaps things weren't so dire after all. I'd been lucky all my life. Maybe I'd get lucky again.

I was lulled into a very mellow mood, and the angry attitude I'd been harboring since my arrival at the hospital began to dissipate. I became reasonable and cooperative, asking as politely as I knew how if I could have something to drink. The nurse obliged with a quarter cup of water, and after swallowing it in a single gulp, I courteously asked for another. And another. And another. I was beginning to get the hang of this. From an environment of complete deprivation, I had been magically transported to a place where, if I asked nicely, I could get whatever I wanted. I tested it out by claiming to still be in pain and was obliged with some powerful sleeping pills. As I drifted off, I gave myself an imaginary pat on the back. I deserved special treatment. I had survived. I was some kind of hero.

I didn't feel like a hero when I woke up the next morning. The drugs had worn off, leaving me as angry and irritable as ever. To make matters worse, I could smell myself. I still hadn't had a shower and, in the stark reality of that morning, the stench was unbearable. I needed some good strong soap and a washcloth to scrub myself clean. I spotted the bathroom door across the room and I started to climb out of bed, when the nurse came rushing in.

"What do you think you're doing?" she demanded.

"I'm taking a shower," I snarled. "Do you mind?" I gestured to the IV in my arm. "You can take this thing out, too. I need some real food."

She pushed me back onto the bed. It was the first time I noticed how weak I really was. "You need to stay put, sir," she said. "Doctor's orders."

"Then get me the doctor," I ordered peremptorily. She didn't know who she was dealing with. I had just survived eight days in the wild. I'd like to see her try it.

She shot me a nasty look and summoned the attending physician on the intercom. A moment later, he entered, looking annoyed. "What seems to be the trouble?"

"I'll tell you what the trouble is, Doc," I said, my sense of entitlement swelling. "I'm starving and I need a shower. How about it?"

"Absolutely not," he replied firmly. "Not in your state."

"And what state is that?" I shot back.

He looked me straight in the eye. "If you eat the wrong thing or experience a sudden change in temperature, you could go into an even more critical state."

I paused, taking in his words. "Are you telling me I'm in critical condition?" I asked, my bluster evaporating.

"Sir," he replied, "you're in intensive care."

He turned abruptly and left the room. The conversation was over and, with it, the heroic self-image I had built up for myself. Instead, a wave of self-pity swept over me. I sank down on the bed, and as I did so, I got a glimpse of my black and swollen feet. I began to cry.

"Look at me," I said to the nurse, in between sobs. "Look what's happened to me." She tucked me in. I don't know if she was trying to hide her emotions or she just didn't have any, but my pathetic state didn't seem to move her in the least.

"Would you like some ice chips?" she asked me as she plumped my pillow.

DEEP INSIDE, I knew I was facing a terrible eventuality. My feet had been badly damaged and the chances were good that the harm was irreparable. But instead of summoning my courage to deal with what, in all likelihood, would be the loss of my feet, I did everything I could to keep the truth buried. I didn't have the ability to cope with what had happened to me. Not yet.

That didn't make me a coward. We all confront life's challenges differently and there is no right way to grapple with tragedy. For some, it comes like a tidal wave that sweeps away everything. For others, it's a rising tide that gets deeper and deeper until you're up to your neck. The result is the same, either way. For me, it was like a leaking dam that sprung more and bigger holes until I couldn't hold it back anymore. That's just the way it happened. If I had been a different person, at a different stage in my life,

I might have handled it better, or worse. But I wasn't and I didn't and I don't make any excuses for that.

Drugs were what I used to plug the leaks in that bursting dam. From that very first day in the hospital, I understood that the painkillers they were giving me worked on more than just the physical level. They also deadened the psychic and spiritual pain I was feeling. Of course, they also put me in a state of suspended animation. As long as I wasn't feeling any pain, I couldn't process what had happened to me, learn to accept it, and find a way to move on. I was stuck, which was all right with me. I had nowhere I wanted to go and no way to get there.

Those around me did the best they could to help, even if they, too, weren't sure how to deal with the situation. There was a fine line between participating in my healing and only feeling pity for me, and I knew it every time that line was crossed. On the morning of my second day in the hospital, for instance, as the news of my rescue began to spread, I got a phone call from my old boss at Easton, where I used to work developing hockey equipment.

"We're all thinking and praying for you here at the office," he said. "And I want you to know that any time you're ready to come back, your old job is waiting for you." I thanked him and hung up, feeling distinctly uncomfortable. I hadn't heard from the guy for years and now, suddenly, he was offering me my old job back? I couldn't help but wonder whether it was because I was a great product developer or he just felt sorry for me. I appreciated the fact that he'd thought enough to call, but I wished he'd been able to keep from sounding so sorry for me. That was the last thing I wanted.

I felt better when members of the rescue team who had conducted the initial manhunt for me came by to introduce themselves and wish me the best. They brought their search dog, a big friendly Labrador, with them, and the presence of that dog was an immediate boost to my spirits. Later that same day, an old friend of mine named Greg Dallas, who runs the mountain and whom I'd once played hockey with, also came by. It was good to see him and, unlike my old boss, he didn't lay on the sympathy too thickly. We were just two buds who had played some great hockey together and had some old times to catch up on.

"When I heard your name on the TV," he said to me, "I told my wife that you were the only one I knew who could have ever made it out of there alive."

But even Greg's visit weighed heavily on my heart. I knew that once he left the hospital, he'd probably be heading back up to the mountain. I had no idea when I'd be able to return.

My parents, of course, were a constant presence, and they did what they could to keep up my spirits. It was difficult for all of us. I knew how worried and frightened they were, and sometimes I found myself wishing that they would just leave me alone until I had a chance to recover. I felt responsible for what they were going through and frustrated that I couldn't simply jump up out of the bed, show them that I was whole and healthy, and return home with them to pick up a new life where I had left off.

That wasn't going to happen. The doctors, who shuttled in and out of my room all day long, made that clear enough. At one point the physician from the U.S. Ski Team was summoned. He brought with him a special device that was used to actually listen deep into my feet for any signs of circulation. His expression at the end of the examination made my heart sink. I felt like telling him the old joke about the horse that walks into the bar. "Why the long face?" the bartender asks. But I didn't. Instead I just lay there as he put his hand on my shoulder and gave me a "poor kid" look. I wanted to kick him in the crotch.

It wasn't until the evening of my second day in the hospital that I was finally cleared to eat. They brought me a tray of beef with mashed potatoes and gravy, some veggies, and a salad. Now, I grew up in the restaurant business and was taught how great food was really supposed to taste. I can make a fine French sauce with the best of them, but I had never in my life tasted a meal as delicious as that plain, ordinary hospital food. After cleaning my plate, I asked for another one and they gave it to me. I polished that one off as well. I then indulged a sudden craving for popsicles and soda pop that I couldn't seem to satisfy. I was on a sugar binge, trying to find a substitute for the instant energy that meth had provided. I could still feel how weak I had become, how my muscles had been eaten away by starvation, and even the temporary boost the sweets gave me was extremely gratifying.

It's amazing what a good meal will do for your general disposition. Once again the world seemed a little brighter and, the doctor's grim prognosis notwithstanding, I felt some of my old optimism returning.

I felt pretty good the next morning, too, when they brought me a huge delicious breakfast of bacon and eggs with all the trimmings. I was just finishing it up when my parents arrived. My dad sat down next to me.

"Eric," he said, "we've been asking around and we're not sure this is the best place for you to be right now. It doesn't seem as if they're really equipped to do everything that needs to be done to try and reverse the frostbite in your feet. We want to transfer you to the Grossman Burn Center. They've done miracles there." *Miracles for what?* I thought.

I tried to ignore the implication that it was going to take a miracle to save my feet. For the moment I was more interested in how a facility dedicated to helping burn survivors could bring back my frozen feet.

Dr. Richard Grossman, a pioneering plastic surgeon who specializes in burn reconstructive surgery and the treatment of what is called "thermal injuries," founded the Grossman Burn Center in 1995 with his son, Dr. Peter Grossman. As the name suggests, "thermal injuries" encompasses damage by both extreme heat and extreme cold. Although the burn center obviously focuses on the former, treating everything from scalding to chemical and electrical burns, it also utilizes some of the same techniques in treating frostbite and the infections that result from frozen tissue. One of the most reputable and successful of such facilities in the world, the burn center brings together a team of top doctors, therapists, psychologists, and caregivers who work to return their patients to the highest level of functioning.

Of course, I had functioned at a very high level and, while I harbored dark doubts that I would ever be able to return to my athletic peak, I trusted the decision that my mom and dad had made. Like them, I suspected that in the small rural hospital where I had been taken, there wasn't the expertise or equipment to give me the best chance for recovery. I would put myself in the hands of the skilled specialists at Grossman.

At the time, I gave no thought to how all this was going to be paid for. Given my condition, I was really only able to focus on whatever was about to happen next. I had no context for understanding what I had been through, or what I was about to go through. Food, water, and pain medication were the extent of my immediate world. My mother had taken out a health insurance policy in my name when I started seriously pursuing extreme snowboarding. I'm not proud of that fact, but I'll always be grateful for her love and foresight when it came to my well-being. By faithfully paying the premiums every month, she was doing for me what I couldn't do for myself, and if it hadn't been for her, I might have been headed for a bed in the charity ward instead of a top medical facility staffed by dedicated professionals.

A nurse came in and started preparing me for the discharge and transfer. I was given the choice of being driven in an ambulance the several hundred miles to my destination or flying down in a special, medically equipped jet. I almost laughed. In my glory days as an athlete, I had often dreamed of traveling from game to game in my own private aircraft. I was finally getting the chance, although in circumstances I could never have imagined.

But I wasn't going anywhere until I had a chance to clean up. However unwillingly, I had given up the right to make many choices in my life. I was, after all, about to put myself in the hands of people I'd never met and knew nothing about. But I was still determined to cling to whatever shred of personal dignity was left to me. I needed a shower and I needed it now.

After some intensive consultation with the doctor, the nurse finally allowed me to get cleaned up. She unhooked the IV, helped me into the bathroom, and then left me to it. A chair had been put under the shower, and I told myself I wasn't going to use it, but I surrendered to the inevitable once the hot water hit my feet and sent a scorching sensation along my injured nerves. I tried to evaluate what was happening: while the tops of my feet were agonizingly sensitive, the bottoms were still completely numb. I found myself wishing that, however intense the pain from the hot water might be, I could experience it on the sole and heels of my feet. It might mean that there was still some life left in them.

There was a knock on the door. "Are you all right in there?" the nurse asked.

"Listen," I replied. "Unless you're willing to come in here with me, I'd appreciate some privacy." That shut her up.

I scrubbed myself vigorously, washing away the clinging odor of piss, pine needles, and sweat that I'd lived with for so long. The water running down my body was comforting and soothing both for my mind and soul.

Two hours later I was on a jet, buzzing from a pain shot, soaring southward over the majestic Sierra Nevada. I could see Mammoth out the window and the huge shadow of the mountain's flank where I had been lost and given up for dead. I was heading for an unknown fate, but the mountain remained, eternal and unconquerable.

CHAPTER FIFTEEN

Whirlpool

BEING SHUTTLED IN a private jet from Mammoth to Southern California gave me the feeling that I was someone special. I was back into the hero mode. I figured I deserved the deluxe treatment I was getting. After all I'd been through, I had it coming to me and it was pretty cool.

It was an impression underscored by our arrival at Van Nuys Airport, where I knew a lot of corporate jets took off and landed. Waiting at the tarmac was an ambulance along with some medical staff, and I was immediately whisked off the plane and into an ambulance waiting for the transfer. I have to admit it: I liked the attention.

But all the high-profile bother and bustle also had another effect on me: a strange sense of utter unreality. As we arrived at the admissions doors of the Grossman Burn Center, where even more physicians and nurses awaited my arrival, it felt to me that I had crossed a line between real life and some kind of fantasy existence. It reminded me of nothing so much as one of those daytime soap operas that take place in a hospital. All the doctors were handsome and all the nurses were pretty, and the room they checked me into was bright and clean and perfectly decorated.

Naturally, I still wasn't quite in my right mind. Everything was happening so quickly, I was still woozy from the pain shots I had taken, and I think I had left behind some part of me back in the raw reality of the mountain. As a result, I felt a weird detachment from all the furious activity around me.

There was also another reason for imagining that I was just playing a part in an unfolding drama. It was another way of insulating myself against the grim actuality of my injuries. As long as I could pretend that this was happening to someone else, then it would be someone else's feet that were in danger of being amputated. I could float above it all, like I'd floated above my own body during that last day on the ridge, or in that jet soaring over the mountain that had nearly killed me. I was a passive observer, nothing more, and I liked it that way.

After I had been evaluated and checked in, they got to work immediately on my feet. There was a comforting assurance in all the efficiency and competence being demonstrated. They knew what they were doing and, while I don't fault the staff at Mammoth Hospital, I've wondered many times whether the outcome might not have been different if I had received that kind of intensive, specialized care during those first two, critical days.

It was my dad who had finally had to step in. As he explained it to me later, "I watched and waited and, when I couldn't take it anymore, I just came out and asked them what their plan was to save your feet. They told me that most of the time frostbite damage would reverse itself. I couldn't accept that. I started checking out alternatives and that's when we found out about Grossman."

One of the features of the burn center's treatment program that especially attracted my dad's attention was their advanced application of what is called a hyperbaric chamber. During his career as a chef, my father had prepared meals for Michael Jackson. "I knew that Michael slept in a hyperbaric chamber," he told me. "I remember him telling me it would keep him young forever. I figured if it was good enough for him, it was good enough for my son."

Often used to treat the decompression sickness of deep-sea divers, a hyperbaric chamber creates a high-pressure, oxygen-rich environment. Healing is promoted by increased oxygen transported through the blood and tissues. It can be used for everything from carbon monoxide poisoning to massive blood loss to, in my case, thermal damage.

I wasn't sure how I felt having medical advice handed down to me from Michael Jackson, but in point of fact, the superstar knew a lot about cutting-edge medical technology in the treatment of burns. After his famous 1984 accident on a TV commercial set, when his hair was set on fire, he became active in providing the funding for what would become known as the Michael Jackson Burn Center in Los Angeles. I wouldn't be surprised if he'd first found out about hyperbaric chambers and oxygen therapy during his own treatment.

I didn't know any of this when the staff at Grossman began to treat me that first day. It was all new to me. They wrapped my feet in gauze and covered them in a kind of fishnet stocking that went halfway up my leg and looked absolutely ludicrous. I got a kick out of lifting up the sheets when my dad came in the room to show him my new cross-dressing look. I was trying to have fun with the whole situation, but I was also fighting a deep fear. No one was making any guarantees and, while the burn center staff were better at hiding their concerns than the doctors and nurses at Mammoth, it was clear to me that I wasn't going to be walking out of there any time soon. This was serious.

As might be expected, I reverted back to drugs to quell my apprehension. Feigning fresh pain, I asked for more meds and they hooked up my IV to a device that I could use to regulate my own dosage. It was like pouring gasoline on a fire. Whenever I started feeling down or sorry for myself or generally out of sorts, I'd press that button for a hit of oblivion. It didn't take long to get to the point that even when I was feeling *good*—hopeful or optimistic—I give myself a dose to enhance the mood. Drugs were the doorway through which I could step in and out of reality at will, and that self-medicating button became the key I would turn again and again to gain entry.

Meanwhile, the effort to save my feet had begun in earnest. Hyperbaric oxygen therapy would be essential to the approach the doctors at Grossman took to restore my circulation and promote the growth of new tissue. Twice a day, for ninety minutes, I would lie down in a small chamber, about the size and dimensions of a futuristic coffin, and let the high-pressure atmosphere do its work. It was hot inside that oxygen-rich tube and I would sweat profusely, but it was a small price to pay for what the doctors hoped would turn around the slow decay of tissue spreading up my ankles. To pass the time, I would watch comedy movies on a small built-in DVD screen, believing that laughter was also good medicine. When I had had enough of *Caddyshack* or *Major Payne,* I'd shoot the breeze through the intercom with Herb, the technician who operated the chamber. Naturally, I nicknamed him Hyperbaric Herb.

When I wasn't getting hyperbaric therapy, I'd oftentimes be subjected to the indignity of what they called the "jacuzzi whirlpool." When I first heard about that part of the treatment, I couldn't wait. At last I'd have the luxury of the long, luxurious soaks I'd dreamed about. Except it turned out to be more like getting sprayed down with a fire hose while strapped to a board. Nurses massaged my feet, trying to force blood down into the shriveled vessels and withered skin, while I endured the torture, humiliated, soaked to the bone, and wearing nothing but a wet towel. I kept telling myself it would all be worth it if I could only get out of there in one piece.

There were other elements of my daily routine that I actually looked forward to. One of the main attractions was eating. I'd inhale five or six meals a day with plenty of snacks in between. I just couldn't stuff in enough food. Since patients were allowed to pick their own menus, I spent long hours poring over the selections, putting together breakfasts, lunches, and dinners in various combinations.

Most of my hours, however, were spent trying not to focus on my feet. It was clear enough just by looking at them that their condition wasn't improving. The dead, black flesh had been steadily encroaching, and one by one, I was losing my toenails. I needed desperately to think about something else. That's when I began to notice that there were others around me in a lot worse shape than I was.

THERE'S A CONSTANT cycle of life and death that goes on in any hospital, a drama that lies just beneath the surface of the daily schedule. To the staff, of course, it becomes part of their job, something they learn to deal with. Their compassion for their patients has to be tempered by the understanding that human beings are fragile and perishable creatures.

I don't think that's anywhere more evident than in a burn unit. There is so much pain and disfigurement that comes from thermal damage that, as the doctors and nurses know only too well, even those who survive are only beginning the struggle to come to terms with their shock and trauma. That's especially true of children, and the Grossman Burn Center was renowned for its treatment of kids. There were six or eight youngsters there at any given time during my stay, and my heart really went out to them. It was especially difficult to see them getting treatment in the hyperbaric chamber. I was a grown man and being inside the narrow tube gave me a claustrophobic, panicky feeling. I could only imagine what those young people, scared and isolated and sometimes in terrible pain, must have been going through.

I was surprised to learn that more than a few patients at the center were Asian kids who had all suffered the same kind of scalding injury, when they had pulled on a kitchen tablecloth and tipped a hot pot of tea on themselves. It was, I was told, a very common kind of burn accident. Others, less frequent, were even more wrenching. One little boy had been badly burned in an apartment fire when his mother, a drug addict, had fallen asleep with a lit cigarette. A little girl's deranged stepfather had locked her in the house and set it on fire. Unbearable tragedies and, sometimes, extraordinary miracles were occurring all around me, and it helped to put my own predicament into perspective.

But it wasn't just the here-and-now that intruded into the everyday routine of that place. Like anywhere else where lives hang in the balance and death is a constant presence, there was an otherworldly aura that was both spiritual and, occasionally, a little spooky. I heard many accounts of patients seeing angels and talking to dead people, and one in particular stays with me to this day. A man named Tony who had been caught in an explosion at his wife's Laundromat and burned over ninety-five percent of his body had been admitted to the intensive care unit, and his wife, Annie, was staying with him day and night. During her vigil, she heard him talking quite clearly, as if he were having a conversation with someone, even though they were alone and he was slipping in and out of consciousness. Tony's wife, distraught by her husband's strange behavior, summoned a nurse, who listened for a while to details of his one-sided dialogue. Tony was talking to a little girl, she finally explained with calm certainty. She had been in a car wreck and had died in a chopper on her way to the burn center. It had happened two years earlier, but Tony seemed to know all about it. Whether he was comforting the child's ghost or it was she who was preparing him for his own journey to the other side is anyone's guess. Suffice it to say, things sometimes got a little weird during the night shift.

Ghost stories and supernatural occurrences contrasted

sharply with the intensely practical and down-to-earth business of treatment and therapy. But there was an invisible connection between them to which I was gradually becoming sensitized. The reality that our bodies are the container for our spirit and that it is the spirit that endures even as the body perishes was a perspective I had never encountered before. My world had been about physical achievement and I gloried in my athletic prowess. It was only when all that was taken away and I was confined to a bed, like a helpless infant returned to the cradle, that the substance of my soul began to emerge at last.

I have always considered myself a good person. Anyone can be good in their own eyes. But I began to understand how that innate goodness had been compromised by my selfishness and ego. It wasn't just that there were others, whose bodies had been scorched and charred in ways far worse than mine, who now surrounded me. For them, the mercy and compassion of a loving God, as expressed in the care and kindness of the staff, were more than just vague abstractions. That was the reality that gave them the strength to go on living. I had always lived for myself and took satisfaction in my stubborn independence. Meth had fueled that isolation and the delusion that I didn't need anyone or anything. I was imbued with the false power of the drug and had become a god in my own eyes. My ordeal on the mountain had shown me otherwise. But the humbling had only just begun.

At the same time that the transformation of my inner

life began, the damage to my body accelerated. When the hyperbaric chamber and other therapies failed to reverse the effects of the frostbite in my feet or the infection that resulted, the doctors decided to try a regimen of stimulants to get my blood flowing again. While the dosages hardly compared to what I had tolerated at the height of my meth addiction, I did feel the familiar boost, the mood elevation that gave me an enhanced but unreal sense of optimism. At a time when it would have been better to prepare for the worst, I persisted in clinging to a false confidence, sure that, somehow, it was all going to work out. When it was decided to give me an angiogram, injecting dye to see if there was any circulation in my lower extremities, I had the surgeon sign one of his rubber gloves. I was so sure that the results of the procedure would be good that I wanted to keep it for a souvenir.

They weren't. Despite the best efforts of some of the most skilled and experienced physicians in the field, my prognosis continued to be grim. In the absence of good news, my positive frame of mind, artificially bolstered by the drugs, began to flag. After nearly a week of intensive therapy, the handwriting was on the wall. But I refused to read it. Instead, I retreated back into myself, sleeping as much as I could and refusing to see the many friends who wanted to come and visit. More than anything, I was afraid to hear the questions I knew they would inevitably ask: How was I doing? What were the doctors saying? When would I be going home? I didn't have the answers to any of them. At least that's what I told myself. The truth was, deep down inside, I knew the reckoning was close at hand. There were consequences to the life I had lived, to the choices I had made, and now the penalty was due.

Was it my drug addiction that was to blame for delivering me to these dreaded dead ends? Was it my arrogance and overconfidence? Meth had clouded my judgment from the moment I woke up that morning to ride the mountain. A belief in my own invulnerability had driven me to head into the wilderness unprepared and underequipped. But can I say for certain that what I was about to go through was the result of my own foolhardiness and conceit?

No, I can't. While I've come to believe that everything happens for a reason and each of our lives has a unique and essential purpose, it's not for me to assign cause and effect to the events that shape our individual destinies. All I can say for certain is what I would later read in the Bible, that God works all things together for good to those who are called by Him.

I was about to hear that call.

CHAPTER SIXTEEN

107.3

I HAD BEEN in intensive care at the Grossman Burn Center almost a week when, one morning after my treatment in the whirlpool, I suddenly became violently ill. I was shaking like a leaf and my teeth were chattering uncontrollably. It was as if all of the bitter cold I had been subjected to on the mountain had been stored up in the marrow of my bones and was suddenly released, radiating a chill that could not be dispelled.

The staff tried their best, cranking up the thermostat in my room and covering me with thick blankets. I was barely conscious of what was happening around me, but I knew enough to realize I had reached the turning point. The infection from my dead feet was starting to spread throughout my body. Gangrene was poisoning me from the inside.

The nurse took my temperature. I clocked in at 107.3 degrees. I was later told that was the highest ever registered at the Grossman Burn Center. In a life that had been defined by extremes, I had finally arrived at the most radical extreme of all. When they had airlifted me off the mountain, my temperature had been a frigid 86. The mercury had now risen a full 21 degrees. I was later told that, given that radical swing, I was fortunate I didn't have a stroke. My body couldn't take much more and I think I would have been a lot worse off if I hadn't been in pretty good shape to begin with.

As my fever rose, the nurses took desperate measures, lifting me on a gurney and wheeling me into an ice-cold bath. If I had been even the slightest bit aware of my surroundings, I'm sure the freezing water would have reminded me of the hockey regimen I'd used in training, where I'd plunge into cold water after a hard workout to reduce the strain and soreness of my muscles by leaching out the lactic acid and enabling a quick recovery. But at that point, I wasn't even sure where I was, much less what was being done to me. I was hallucinating, seeing frightening faces and hearing uncanny sounds, as if all the ghosts that lurked in the halls of the hospital had come to welcome me to their netherworld.

After they had managed to lower my temperature a bit, they took me back to my bed. I was still trembling between chills and fever and had become unbearably sensitive to the slightest stimulation. The glare of the blaring TV was too much to tolerate, and the light from the win-

dow glanced off the metal surfaces of the medical equipment with blinding intensity. I was starting to think a little
more clearly, but there was only one recurring thought
that chased itself through my mind: I was in trouble.
Fearful and alone, I wanted to retreat into the darkness of
my room and hide from what was about to happen.

But there was no escape. That evening a doctor came
in alone and, after a quick examination, informed me that
they were going to have to perform emergency amputation surgery as soon as possible. It was my worst fear and
he delivered the horrifying news in a tone of voice devoid
of emotion. "Don't you care?" I wanted to scream in his
face. "Don't you even give a damn?" But I know now that
for him, as for every doctor and nurse in that place, a
seeming lack of feeling was the only way they had to protect themselves against the anguish and sorrow that was
so often a part of their jobs.

But I had no such protection. I was left alone to fight a
losing battle against despair and stark fear. After the doctor left to prepare for the operation, I sat up in bed and
stared at my feet for a long time. I started pulling at the
fishnet stockings and suddenly found myself tearing them
away and unwrapping my bandages until I could see the
blackened and blistered flesh for myself. I started rubbing
my toes, my feet, my ankles, trying to restore their life any
way I could. A wave of self-recrimination swept over me.
You're pathetic, I told myself over and over. *How could you let*

this happen to you? I wanted to blame God, the mountain, the meth, but in the end it was only my fault. I was going to lose my feet, and the long-delayed recognition of that inevitability was too much to contain. I groaned a sound that came from the depths of my soul, beyond words, raw and guttural. I would never be the man I was again. I wouldn't be a man at all. Instead, I was going to be a freak, a cripple, an object of scorn.

There's another passage in the Bible that would later give me a lot of comfort and consolation. It says that God will never bring us more suffering than we can bear. Today, I believe that with all my heart. But in that hospital bed, waiting for them to come and chop my feet off, no one could have reassured me that I had the strength to endure the ordeal I was about to suffer. It was a crushing weight and I could hardly breathe beneath it.

Sometime during that evening, Rick, an old friend of mine, arrived to visit. He loved sports as much as I did, and we had surfed and ridden and torn up the ice together on a regular basis. If I'd known he was going to come, I would have told the staff at nurses' station to keep him out, but by the time he showed it was too late to turn him away. When he found out what was going to happen to me, he began pacing the room back and forth, muttering to himself, until I couldn't stand it anymore.

"Just go home," I told him. "It's going to be okay." I was surprised at the sincerity in my voice. In that moment, I truly wanted to provide some solace for my anguished

friend. Maybe it helped a little to relieve my own trepidation.

But not for long. After my friend left, I lay in the
gloom of the darkened room, my thoughts full of futility
and self-loathing. After a few minutes I became aware of a
low murmur in the hallway outside. Three nurses had
gathered to chat and, while it was hard to make out the
words, the pitying pitch of the voices made it completely
clear what they were discussing.

"Hey!" I shouted, my anger and frustration welling up
again. "I know what you're talking about! Why don't you
mind your own business?" Embarrassed, one of them shut
the door, plunging the room even deeper into shadows.

I closed my eyes and buried my face in the pillow. All I
wanted to do was sleep—sleep for a thousand years. But
when sleep finally came, it brought no rest. Instead, I was
haunted by nightmares and the voices and visages that increasingly intruded into my fevered state of mind as the
infection spread through my wracked body. It seemed as if
I were hovering that night between two worlds, the living
and the dead, and the boundary between had become
blurred and permeable. Cackling laughter mixed with ago-
nized moans. Whispers mingled with screams. The walls
seemed to bend outwards and vaporous figures floated in
and out of my room. I saw mountains looming over me,
dissolving into a blizzard of images and impressions: the
glinting eyes of a wolf, the smack of a twig on a puck, the
thundering of a waterfall and the cheers of an Olympic

crowd. I was everywhere and nowhere, reliving my life through a warped prism, experiencing all the highs and lows in one relentless rush that took me nowhere.

I awoke with a start, instantly aware of where I was and what was about to happen. I sensed a presence in the room with me and turned to see my mother sitting at my bedside. I had no idea how long she had been there, but from the dim light through the closed window blinds, I knew it was very early in the morning.

My eyes filled with tears. "Mom," I said, choking back a sob. "I can't do this. I can't go through with it. I'm not ready yet." I had the same panicked feeling I'd get when I was unprepared for a big hockey game, as if I still needed my ritual pregame nap, meal, and workout routine.

She began to speak, softly and tenderly, and more than the words she said, it was the way she said them that brought me a sense of peace and a slow but sure acceptance of what had to happen. I asked her later what she had said that had made such a difference that morning.

"I can't exactly remember, either," she admitted. "I told you that I loved you, of course. I told you that I hadn't lost you on that mountain and I wasn't going to lose you to a fever. But to tell you the truth, I don't think it was anything so special. It was just being there, together, the two of us, that somehow felt right. You needed me then, and I needed to be there. That was enough."

It was more than enough. What I remember most, in the dimness of that room, was my mother's eyes, calm and compassionate, giving me strength where I had none, letting her love and courage and faith fill the empty places inside me. People can argue all they want about whether angels are real. All I know is that, sometimes, human beings are available at a special time in a certain place to do God's will.

THERE WERE A lot of angels on hand in the hours leading up to my operation, along with a few others who were only too human. Rebecca Grossman, Dr. Peter Grossman's wife, came by my room to bring me some inspirational tapes that would prove to be important in my recovery in the first weeks after the amputation. At one point, after I had drifted off to sleep again, I woke to find Dr. Grossman himself standing at the foot of my bed, his hands on my feet, deep in thought and prayer. I'll never forget the compassion I saw in his face when our eyes met. A family friend came by briefly to drop off a CD that included a song called "Point My Feet." It gave me a surge of hope and optimism so heartening that I requested it to be played in the operating room during the surgery. As Eminem's "Soldier" had been for me on the mountain, so that song of worship became my anthem in the hospital.

These were all authentic miracles in my mind, small acts of human kindness that touched a place deep inside of me that had for so long been crystallized. I can't say I saw God's hand in the way people seemed to arrive at just the right moment, with just the right gifts of encouragement. I hadn't really made that connection yet. All I knew was that I had a renewed assurance that, no matter what the outcome would be, my life would go on. I would find a new purpose and new direction, and I clung to that certainty like I had clung to the rocks as the river had swept me toward Rainbow Falls.

But, as I said, not everyone I encountered that morning was a ray of pure sunshine. The orderly who came to take me to the operating room handled me like a sack of potatoes and stank of cigarettes.

"Ready?" he asked me when he was done.

Shut the hell up! I wanted to shout. *Would you be ready if they were going to cut your feet off?*

But he was nothing compared with the surgeon who performed the complex and demanding procedure. I was told he was the best in the field, but his bedside manner left a lot to be desired. No matter how many times I saw him afterwards, he always looked the same: weedy gray hair fringing his bald head in a classic mad-scientist mode and a pair of black cowboy boots that made him look even taller than his cadaverous six-foot-six frame. He spoke in bone-dry medical terminology that I couldn't begin to understand and had a personality to match—aloof and utterly detached.

As I had requested, "Point My Feet" was being played as I was being put under, and the words and melody were still resonating when I woke up in the Intensive Recovery

Unit a few hours later. I opened my eyes and looked around, even as the uplifting song began to fade in my ears with a deadening echo. I was alone; alone with the disorientation and confusion that come from the aftereffects of anesthesia; alone to cope with what had been taken from me while I was dead to the world.

I looked down the length of my body toward the far end of the bed. There, where my feet would normally have tented the sheets, my legs abruptly ended just above my ankles. It had happened. The process that had begun that first night on the back side of Mammoth Mountain had reached its terrible end. My feet were gone and, with them, a huge part of who I was.

I cried without shame, without fear that someone would come in and discover me sobbing like a baby. I was grieving for more than just the loss of part of my physical frame. I was grieving for the loss of all the places my feet had taken me, all the walking and running and skating and snowboarding I had done without even thinking about it. It may seem strange, even silly, but I regretted the fact that I hadn't said goodbye to them, blown a kiss to my toes and my ankles and my heels and my soles. They were beautiful, more beautiful than I'd ever realized. I had taken them for granted, the way we all take our bodies and the marvelous parts that work so wondrously together for granted. I would have given anything to have them back, just one more time, to appreciate one last time how the muscles and bones and tendons were knit together, to flex the joints and wiggle the digits and let them do all the things that feet can do. "Where did they go?" I wondered to myself. "What happened to them?" And fresh tears flowed.

The pain that I was feeling was deep and abiding, but it was psychic suffering, not physical. The aftermath of the amputation was being dealt with by massive infusions of painkillers, which I could administer at will with a push of the button that was connected to the IV hooked directly into my chest through a main line. The drug dependency that I'd been developing since coming to the burn center was now magnified and multiplied as I used the pain medication to block out the terrible truth of my maimed body. It didn't matter that the medications gave me a pounding headache or left me severely constipated. That was a price I was happy to pay in exchange for the stupor they induced.

I loved the feeling of being high. It was there that I hovered for several days after my surgery, dazed and drowsy, sleeping for hours when I wasn't staring absently out the window. Whenever I felt the slightest flicker of emotion, good, bad, or indifferent, I would hit that button and away it would go. Of course, the staff did its best to control my drug intake, but by complaining loudly about the pain I was feeling, I was able to keep the supply flowing freely.

And it always did the trick, until it didn't. Slowly, of course, I began to build up a tolerance, even for the most powerful of the painkillers they had available, and I began to develop secretive methods to enhance my high. I would chew up the time-release pills they gave me to release the full narcotic effect all at once, and I soon figured out how to override the cutoff on the IV by jamming a pencil into the self-medicating device. I was both bold and devious in my attempts to avoid facing my dilemma, and I stubbornly resisted the best efforts of the staff to begin the rehabilitation process.

As part of my therapy I was encouraged to go to a burn survivors' support group that was held at the burn center. It was a way for patients to share their experience and help one another through the difficult first days after the loss of a limb or other disfigurement. But I wanted nothing to do with it. Regardless of my condition, I still considered myself a world-class athlete and an Olympic champion. The shameful truth was, I clung to the illusion that I was superior to the other survivors who had already admitted that they couldn't work out their problems on their own. I didn't need help. I didn't want help. And I wasn't available to help anyone else.

As reprehensible as that pride and arrogance might seem, it was the only way I had, outside of drugs, to deal with the loss of my feet. I had been diminished, in stature and spirit, and I needed to pump myself up to compensate for my loss. It was an attitude that often expressed itself in bravado. If others believed that I didn't care, that I could shrug it off, maybe I'd believe it myself. I sometimes used humor to get the point across that I was on top of the situation.

"Hey, have you seen my feet?" I'd ask the nurses and staff when they came on their rounds. "There's a left and a right, about size ten, kind of hairy, kind of smelly." They'd chuckle and for a moment I actually did feel better. Laughing was therapeutic, for them and for me.

But it didn't last long and reality bore down as my days in the burn center turned to weeks. I began to obsess over what had actually been done with my feet. Alone at night, I'd have vivid fantasies of a chamber of horrors deep in the bowels of the hospital where severed limbs floated in giant vats of formaldehyde. It haunted me, as if I had misplaced a part of myself and could not rest easy until I found it. I was only half joking when I asked the gaunt and dour doctor with the cowboy boots what he had done with my feet. He sputtered out a flustered reply about incinerating body parts, and I felt a grim satisfaction in having made him so uncomfortable. It was a small act of revenge against the man who had mutilated me without a second thought.

Yet, sometimes it didn't feel as if my feet were gone at all. It is a common phenomenon known as "phantom limb syndrome" and is familiar to many amputees. When an arm or a leg is suddenly lost, the nerves take much longer than flesh and bone to recover and can often send off sharp electrical shocks that feel as if they are originating directly from the missing limb. While I experienced this eerie and uncomfortable sensation, I was fortunate that it didn't persist. Some amputees who suffer abrupt loss from accidents or explosions can feel these mysterious pains for a lifetime, as if being constantly reminded of the part of them that is missing, waking in screaming pain.

Another troubling side effect of amputation, especially when the lower limbs are involved, is a measurable rise in body temperature. With less area to circulate through, the blood can't as effectively disperse our natural heat. Feet in particular are vital in this process because of the distance blood has to travel to reach them. That's one reason our feet sweat so much: they are a natural regulator of our internal temperature. As a result, an amputee can have the sensation of being as much as thirty percent hotter than a person with all their limbs, and to this day my head and neck always seem to be several degrees warmer, as if they are trying to compensate for my decreased body mass. I sweat constantly—even just standing. It became hard for me to tolerate a room heated higher than seventy-two degrees, a fact my poor family would have difficulty adjusting to.

Such physiological changes would have been difficult enough to face without the severe mental and emotional strains that accompany amputation. But for someone like me, defined almost solely by my physical prowess, there was no discernible difference between the physical and the psychological. When my feet had been cut away, a part of my soul had been sliced off, too. I might never find my feet again. But the search for the missing part of my soul had just begun.

CHAPTER SEVENTEEN

Wheelies

TEN DAYS AFTER my amputation surgery, the doctors determined that I needed another operation. It was part of a complex medical calculation that took into account how I could best be fitted for prosthetics. Since I was a bilateral BK (Below Knee) amputee, my legs needed to be as symmetrical as possible to ensure that the artificial graphite and carbon limbs I received would work as well as possible in conjunction with what remained of the muscles and bones below my knees. They had to cut eight inches more from below my knees to make better use of my truncated calf muscles.

Looking back, I wish I had opted for keeping as much of my real legs as I possibly could. There was a procedure that would have fused the two remaining bones to create a plateau along with more muscular control, more stability for the prosthesis, and less sensitivity with the ridge fittings. It would have given me a better result. But I can hardly blame the doctors for moving ahead with the accepted method. I gave them absolutely no input. Instead, I refused to even consider what my choices were. I had given no thought at all to using prosthetics. Like going to the burn survivor support meetings, it was just one more step down a road that I didn't want to travel. It was one thing to have my feet removed. It was another to try and adapt to a poor substitute for the real thing. I saw myself hobbling around on stiff unyielding planks and shuddered at the thought of the pity people would take on me. I didn't want to be treated differently from anyone else. It's the way everyone in a challenged situation feels. We only want to be treated equally. But as long as I denied my condition—both the limitations it posed and the potential it offered for another kind of life—I *was* different. The bottom line was, no one felt as sorry for me as I did.

My second operation lasted ten full hours. I was under deep anesthesia the entire time, and when I finally came to, the first thing I was aware of was how sore my throat was. I had had an oxygen tube run down my esophagus for the duration, and the resulting irritation made it difficult to swallow or even take a deep breath. But my problems were just beginning. As I slowly came back from my comatose condition, I felt a stabbing pain on the shin of my right leg, just at the point where they had operated. I pulled back the blankets to see what was causing it. Both my legs had been placed into tightly fitting casts to control the swelling, and the casts had been butted up against the open wounds just below my knees with a snug garter belt.

I was familiar with garter belts from my time as a hockey player. Players used them to hold up the socks that they pull over their shin pads. But they weren't some kind of fancy high-tech equipment. In fact, the ones favored by most players were the old-fashioned elastic variety that utilized sharp-toothed metallic clips—the same kind that was now holding the casts securely to my skin. The problem was, the cast had been molded into my shin and was pressing into the bone of my shin; it was a constant biting. I summoned a nurse and told her what the problem was, but because the entire rig was already in place, they were reluctant to detach it. More than a week would pass before they finally removed the cast and relieved that throbbing ache.

The days immediately after my second operation marked a sharp decline in my mental and emotional state. I was still on pain medication, of course, but instead of transporting me to the fluffy pink clouds where I floated serenely in the early days after my rescue, I was living in a tinderbox world that could ignite my uncontrollable rage at a moment's notice. I kept an eagle eye on the clock in my room and was sure to inform the nurse five minutes before my meds were due to be administered.

It's a state of mind familiar to anyone who has ever experienced the depths of an addiction to painkillers. Everything is fine, perfect in fact, as long as all your exacting requirements are met, your slightest wish is granted, and your every need and desire anticipated. But if, God forbid, someone falls short of your expectations, you feel fully justified in lashing out and throwing a full-blown temper tantrum, verbally and even physically abusing anyone who has disrupted the delicate balance of your well-being.

It's a profoundly selfish state of mind and one that is wholly dedicated to a single overriding aim: maintaining your high. And if someone or something should send a ripple across that calm, shallow puddle of tranquility, there is hell to pay. It was a condition that fed all too easily into my own desperate attempts to prop up my ego. I had been living for myself and myself alone for so long that it was an easy step to allow the drugs to fuel a sense of entitlement. I had suffered enough. The world owed me. It was payback time.

What was really happening, of course, was that the anger and grief and incomprehensible sense of loss that I had suppressed for so long were finally beginning to break through. I wouldn't allow myself to acknowledge that the life I had lived was over and that I needed to begin a new one. I couldn't face what had happened. So it turned to face me, with a ferocious intensity that overwhelmed everything.

There were certain medications that twisted my thoughts and feelings into grotesque masks of arrogance and anger. Percocet was one of the worst and my reaction to it was so severe that my friends and family would often ask, "Is he on the blue pills?" If I was, they would turn around and go home.

The staff itself learned quickly to be wary of me, but at the same time had been trained not to take abuse, no matter how high I heaped it. At one point, shortly after my second operation, the food that was being provided didn't measure up to my high standards. I made my displeasure known to the nurse, who was decidedly underwhelmed by my whining. Outraged at her audacity, I threw the dinner tray at her. She deftly ducked it and left the room, shutting the door behind her. The mess I had made remained strewn across the floor for the next twenty-four hours. It was the hospital's not-so-subtle way of reminding me who was in charge.

When I wasn't giving vent to my towering rages, I was indulging my increasing fixation on being recompensed for my loss. I would spend hours at a time poring over glossy magazines, cutting out pictures of luxury cars and high-end stereo equipment and every other expensive extravagance that caught my eye. Gathering all my clippings, I'd paste them together to create elaborate collages mirroring my rampant fantasies of wealth and privilege. This is what I wanted now. This is what I deserved. I had lost my feet, but no one could take away a flash Mercedes or a sixty-five-inch flat screen. I was going to get something out of all that I had been through.

The high point of my hospital stay was when I received a visit from hockey superstar Wayne Gretzky. A humble man with a generous spirit, Gretzky had simply dropped by to express solidarity with a fellow player, but the visit turned into a major media event and I took it to mean that my new career as an inspirational icon was getting under way. But I also felt embarrassed as the meds caused me to drift in and out of consciousness.

"I'm sorry," I said to Gretzky. "I just can't focus right now."

"Don't worry about it," he replied. "I'm just happy to have a chance to visit with you. You're a testament to the toughness of hockey players everywhere."

Not long afterwards the hospital arranged for a news conference in response to the crush of requests from media outlets. I dressed in my old hockey jersey for the occasion, but I was so high I barely remember the event. It was just a blur of shouted questions and clicking camera shutters. But I do remember one thing. I did an interview in French with a European reporter and when asked by a reporter what my plans for the future were, I leaned forward into the microphones and, without thinking about it, made a prediction. "I'm going to go snowboarding again. By next season I will be on the mountain again," I told the assembled crowd.

A moment of silence passed as I looked out across the assembled faces, which included several of my friends and former teammates. I could read the skepticism, the disbelief, and, of course, the pity. No one believed I would ever get back on a board again, much less take a run through pure powder with the fresh alpine air blowing in my face, surrounded by the grandeur of the mountain.

No one, that is, but me.

* * *

DESPITE THE HOLE of drug addiction I had dug for myself; despite the self-loathing I nurtured and the rage at the world I had unleashed; despite the stubborn rejection of reality that I clung to like a drowning man; despite it all, there was still a spark of resolve and resolution and sheer dogged determination that flickered in my ravaged mind and body. It was as if my grandfather had suddenly emerged from my past to remind me of what I was capable of doing. People are never completely one thing or the other. None of us is entirely good, or utterly evil. We love and hate in equal measure. We are inconsistent, unpredictable, and contradictory. That's what makes us human. My human nature expressed itself without restraint during those dark days after I lost my feet. I was cruel and selfish, to be sure. But I had a residue of courage, too, and a sense of my own worth that had always served me well. A part of me had given up on myself. But another part of me would never give up.

The days I spent recovering at the burn center were occupied with staying high, taking advantage of my new star status, and plotting my life of fame and fortune. But the nights were different. The nights were quiet and lonely, haunted by the ghosts of that place and lit only by the dim glow from the nurses' station. I slept when I could, as much as I could, and when sleep eluded me I would lie awake, alone with my thoughts and fears.

But after a while, there are only so many angles from which you can think over the same thing and so many fears that can jump out at you like Halloween ghouls. After a while, I got tired of just lying there, listening to the same endless repetitive loop of my mind. I got restless and bored. I needed something else to do. I needed a workout.

As I slowly tried to heal, I asked for an overhead support bar to assist me in sitting up and down and getting in and out of bed. Before long I was doing one hundred pull-ups a day with it. I was provided with a wheelchair to have more mobility within the confines of the hospital. I was soon stretching the envelope of what was allowed and what wasn't. Initially, I roamed the halls in the middle of the night for hours on my own, exploring every nook and cranny of the place and always half expecting to discover that secret House of Horrors room where they kept all the severed arms and legs.

It felt great to have a modicum of my old independence back, and to be able to get some decent exercise for my upper body. As I worked up a sweat, I could feel some strength returning to my arms and shoulders, and it was only then that I fully realized how debilitated my ordeal had left me. The drugs had done their damage, of course, and so had the long weeks I'd spent virtually immobile in bed. But I could sense that the fatigue and weakness were more a result of what I had endured during my eight days and nights on the mountain. I had reached my limit and then somehow pushed beyond, and it was going to take a lot of concentrated effort, especially without my feet, to get back in shape.

But I was bound and determined to do just that. Something small yet significant had clicked inside me that day at the press conference. I might have surprised myself as much as anyone else by declaring that I would return to the snowboarding slopes. But I had meant it and I knew it to be true. All my life I had been dedicated to the pursuit of goals, from the NHL to the Olympics and beyond. Every goal I made, and every jump I completed, was an expression of that quest. It was what made me tick, and my spirit had responded with what felt like a joyous leap when I blurted out my intention to the press and my friends and family. As it turned out, I wasn't quite ready to give up the best part of who I was.

It didn't take long for me to look for something more challenging than the empty hallways of the hospital. I found it when, on one of my midnight rambles, I came across a ramp that led down to the ambulance loading dock near the emergency room. For the next several nights, I would repeatedly wheel myself to the top of the incline, ride down, and then do it all over again. I was getting a double benefit: the training that came from pulling myself up that long steep slope and the sensation of speed I got from rolling down as fast as I could, popping wheelies the whole way. Some things never change. I was still an adrenaline junkie. For the first time since I'd arrived at the facility, I felt like I was accomplishing something significant. I would keep at it until the meds were due or the nurses came looking for me to begin my morning therapy.

I didn't appreciate being tracked down like an escaped convict, which was exactly how I was beginning to feel. With my new freedom of movement, I decided to make a break for it. One morning, I wheeled myself out of the hospital and headed across the street to a neighboring computer store to look over some of the latest laptop models. I ended up ordering forty-eight hundred dollars' worth of equipment.

"My name is Eric Le Marque," I told the clerk, "and I'm staying across the street at the burn center."

On the way back I decided to take a shortcut across the lawn, but my inexperience in navigating less-than-ideal surfaces caused me to flip over. I was filthy, covered in mud, and had put myself at risk of even greater infection. I waited, angry and humiliated, until a staffer who had seen the whole thing came down and got me. After that they took away the wheelchair for a few days until I promised to behave myself.

Before I was finally discharged, I would spend two and a half months at the Grossman Burn Center trying to recover from my amputation. My wounds stubbornly refused to close, despite the best efforts of the staff to promote healing through long sessions in the hyperbaric chamber and the use of powerful antibiotics. It was an indication of just how compromised my body had become that I was abnormally prone to infection, and even after I was released, I was forced to wear a clumsy and noisy pumping device that sucked out fluids from the affected areas.

It didn't work. Aside from having to return three or four times a week for therapy, I would be brought back to the burn center twice more for extended stays in the months to come. I was battling a very serious staph infection that often occurs in individuals with a compromised immune system. I was having prolonged difficulties adjusting to the prostheses I had been fitted with. No matter how much they helped to regain my ability to walk, I resented the fact that I had to wear them at all. I felt clumsy and awkward and the muscles it took to control them properly were constantly sore and overworked. Despite my best efforts to improve my physical condition, I felt as if I were sliding in the other direction.

It was proving increasingly difficult to keep my spirits up. I tried to maintain an exercise regimen, but more often than not couldn't really see the point of continuing. Being discharged from the hospital, away from the constant care that had been provided, only made me feel more frightened and alone. Once again, I lapsed into self-loathing. I may have accomplished a great feat by escaping the mountain alive. But I had not escaped unscathed. I had been a great athlete, a conqueror of worlds, a well-known sportsman who was a legend in my own mind. Now I was reduced to limping around on artificial feet, lugging a machine behind me to suck the pus out of my unhealed wounds, making loud embarrassing noises. I began to be plagued by the thought that it might have been better if I had died on the mountain after all.

CHAPTER EIGHTEEN

Poor Johnny

FINALLY LEAVING THE Grossman Burn Center after almost ten weeks brought with it a mix of tumultuous emotions. The place had become a home for me, a sanctuary from a world that I no longer knew how to navigate. As much as I yearned to be free from the structures and strictures of the hospital and to reclaim as much of my independence as I could manage, I also had deep trepidation about what was waiting for me on the other side of those discharge doors. "Who is going to take care of me now?" I wondered.

My dependency on painkillers had become as entrenched as my earlier addiction to meth, and it was hard to imagine what life would be like without recourse to the array of pills that was provided to me on demand. In fact, I was still in a great deal of pain as my body tried to adjust to the traumatic changes it had undergone.

Aside from my ongoing medical dilemma, I had to deal

with the financial ramifications of my long convalescence. At one point, my mother went to pick up antibiotics for me at the pharmacy. Due to some snarled paperwork, my insurance coverage was denied and she was charged the full amount for the medicine.

"They want twelve hundred dollars," she told me in a frantic phone call. "Eric, I can't afford it. I'm going to have to take out another mortgage on the house."

We eventually got the mistake cleared up but the hassles with insurance companies and the health care providers were enough to drive me deeper into despair and drug abuse.

Meanwhile, I was still confined to a wheelchair. My amputation wounds were infected and the prosthetic legs were not yet an option. When I was finally fitted for them, getting accustomed to their use would be a constant challenge. I had asked that they be made to my playing height on skates. I had always wanted to be taller than I was, and this seemed like a good opportunity to top six feet. But I hadn't anticipated how my enhanced stature would make me feel like I was balancing on stilts or how it would redistribute my weight in ways that put extra stress on my joints and muscles. I began to suffer from frequent pains.

Suffice it to say, there were good reasons to resort to medication to help ease the physical symptoms I was suffering, but of course, that was only a small part of the reason for my continued heavy reliance on prescription drugs once I left the hospital. The real pain I was experiencing was in my heart and my mind and my spirit. If I wasn't going to be a champion athlete anymore, I had no way of knowing who I was or what I was going to do with the rest of my life. Simply put, I had no Plan B and, in the absence of a purpose or goal to strive for, a dark void had opened up at my core.

I've heard it said that anger is a way that we express our depression. I'm not sure whether I was more motivated by rage or despondency, but it didn't make much difference. I was all the same big bundle of misery, and since I couldn't contain it in myself, I let loose on those closest to me.

I had returned to live with my mother after leaving the hospital, and while it was good to be back in familiar surroundings, I was hardly picking up where I'd left off. An eternity had passed since I had last come through that door, the day I had left for Mammoth Mountain. There was something profoundly disheartening about returning to the remnants of the life I used to have. My stuff was there, just as I had left it: the clothes in the closet and my sports equipment waiting and ready. I saw it all now through new eyes, a life out of order and thrown together. *What a mess,* I thought.

The plaques, team photos, medals, and trophies I had gathered throughout my career were still on display, but now they were no longer a source of pride. Instead, they only served to remind me of what I had lost. It was as if I was now occupying the room of another person, someone I was once proud of being and who was now a stranger to me.

At the same time, I was becoming a stranger to those around me. My mom did her best to accommodate me, helping any way she could with my medical needs and trying her best to overlook my radical mood swings. It was a difficult and demanding task, even for a loving mother, and I did nothing to ease her burden. In my frequent black moods, I would verbally abuse her, demanding constant attention and flying into an uncontrolled fury if she didn't perform the menial tasks I required to my satisfaction. I remember being particularly peeved that she hadn't fitted out my room with all the special medical equipment I had had at the hospital. "They gave you a list!" I screamed.

When words weren't sufficient to express my disgust and despair with myself and with everything around me, I resorted to violence, throwing anything I could get my hands on against the nearest wall. I hurled food, furniture, and sometimes even myself, all in a frenzied attempt to destroy what I could no longer control. Twice, in the depths of my anger, I fell out of my wheelchair, twice jumping from a car and injuring myself so seriously that further surgery was required to repair the sutures I had torn out. I was unequipped emotionally and mentally to deal with the transition I was facing. As a consequence, I was forced into a kind of accelerated process of growing up, one that had been delayed ever since I had given up a normal childhood to pursue my professional hockey dreams. Of necessity, that maturing process began at almost the infancy stage. I was like a baby who couldn't get what I wanted and had no self-control or internal discipline. I wanted to be independent, to do everything by myself, but at the same time I wanted to be taken care of, coddled and cosseted. I oscillated wildly between those two extremes, angry that no one could understand what I was going through, but at the same time unwilling to even try to express my feelings and frustrations to anyone.

It wasn't just my mother who bore the brunt of my wrath. My friends, too, did what they could to help me, only to be rewarded with my impatience and scorn. The fact was, none of them really knew how to best support a person in my situation. They wanted to be of assistance, but they ended up either doing too much and making me feel like a helpless invalid, or doing too little and leaving me in the lurch. There were more than a few times when one of my old snowboarding partners would volunteer to take me to the burn center for an appointment, only to drop me off and then drive away, leaving me to navigate the curbs and doorways by myself in a wheelchair.

But what really pushed my buttons was their pitying attitude. It expressed itself in what I called a "poor Johnny pat," on the top of my head, as if I were a helpless child. Once, when a friend did it, I whirled around in my wheelchair and glared at him. "Dude," I said, "did you just give me a 'poor Johnny'? Because if you did, let me tell you something: I can still kick your ass!"

I can't really blame them. For the most part, they were jocks, and I, of course, had been the jock's jock. They were unfamiliar and uncomfortable with the requirements of a physically challenged person. Our credo had been to overcome any physical challenge. That's what we reveled in. Now here I was, as helpless and stubborn as a toddler, and they simply didn't know how to deal with it or to make allowances outside their own comfort zone.

So I tried to deal with it myself, at least for a little while. My strategy was simple, and, in retrospect, simpleminded. I would just make believe that nothing had changed. I'd hang out with my crew the way I used to, partying and pushing the limits and pretending that the good old days had never come to an end.

The whole scheme came crashing down one night shortly after I'd left the hospital, when I went over to the house of one of my friends up in Malibu Canyon. Sure enough, the usual suspects were gathered, and they even helped carry me up the stairs to where a bong was being passed around. I sat on the couch and took a couple of hits.

Twenty minutes later I was in the bathroom, standing on my knees and staring at myself in a full-length mirror, horrified at how short I was. The pot had made things worse, much worse. The enhanced perception that had once made the world so trippy and tangible had now turned into an unsparing microscope that I was squirming under. It was as if I were staring at a creature from some hellish medieval landscape in that mirror—a freak, an abomination. I remembered that old anti-drug ad on TV that compared being high to your brain frying an egg, and I could almost feel my synapses sizzling as I gazed at my reflection. With a strangled cry I crawled back into the living room and had my friends carry me back to my wheelchair. I wheeled myself the four miles along the back roads of Malibu Canyon to my mother's house, a three-hour journey, to sweat out the terrifying effects of the drug. It was the last time I ever let myself believe that I could ignore what had happened to me. And the last time I would ever smoke weed.

It wasn't going to be so easy to forget what I had lost. Nor was it easy to forgive myself, or others. As I struggled to come to terms with the destruction of my old identity, those closest to me were fighting battles of their own.

"I had to learn a lot of self-control," my mother explains. "It was hard, after a while, not to feel resentful. I was doing everything I could to help you and it didn't seem to matter. There was just no way to reach the hurt you were feeling inside. And in the worst times, it hurt me, too, when I wondered whether it wouldn't have been better if God had just taken you on that mountain."

THE SITUATION CAME to a head several months after I had returned from the burn center. It was after a particularly horrendous outburst and my mother had taken as much as she could stand. Over my objections, she loaded me in the car and drove out to the beach. Together we made our way across the boardwalk and watched the slow-rolling surf come in. The soothing rhythm of the waves had the effect she had hoped for: slowly but steadily, some of my unreasoning rage began to leak away.

I had always loved the ocean. Despite the fact that I regularly challenged the waves at many of the best surf spots in Southern California, the sun and salt air stirred a sense of peace and tranquility in me. That day, as I silently watched the white specks of sails against the horizon, with my mother at my side, I found my way back toward that calm center. I could see the big picture for the first time in as long as I could remember. My problems had become the whole of my existence. I was trapped in a labyrinth of feeling and thoughts that circled in on itself ever more tightly. But the world beyond still turned, the tides still ebbed and flowed, and the sun and moon rose and set as regular as clockwork. There was a comfort in realizing that again. It was an assurance that, no matter how bad it seemed, life had a way of going on, with or without you.

"Mom, I'm sorry," I said as the sun sank low over the western water.

"Eric," she replied, "don't say another thing. I love you and I know you will overcome this."

They were just the right words, at just the right time. I leaned my head on her shoulder in the golden light of the fading day.

Returning home that evening, I made a few decisions

that I had put off for a long time. The first was to finally attend a support group for amputees. I can't say that gathering with others in my situation and hearing their stories was exactly the solution I was looking for. As it turned out, I would go to such meetings only a few times. But as brief as my encounter was, it helped me in at least beginning to take the first faltering steps toward restoration. Maybe I was still too independent, a character trait that has both good and bad aspects to it. I had never been much of a joiner. But it was the choice I had made to go meet with others who shared my experience that was so significant. It was an admission, unspoken perhaps but nonetheless real, that I couldn't handle this by myself. I had been putting myself and others through a horrific ordeal, but I was at last moving onward from being a child, thinking I could do it all myself, to being a man, acknowledging that sometimes it's okay to ask for help. It didn't happen all at once, and for every step forward that I took, there were two steps in the other direction. But it was still progress.

The second decision I made at the end of that day on the beach would have much more lasting and profound repercussions. It was true that, after my ordeal on the mountain, most of my time was spent feeling sorry for myself and pissed off at the world. But there were other times, especially late at night, when the effects of the painkillers had begun to wear off and I was awake with my own thoughts, when I would ponder the deeper meaning of everything that had happened to me.

Was there a reason I had gone through this devastating tribulation? Why had everything that seemed so important to me been suddenly snatched away? Would I ever discover another purpose as fulfilling as the physical accomplishments that had made me who I was?

I didn't know the answer to those questions, but it seemed to me that, by asking them, at least I was being honest with myself. There was no longer any percentage in hoping for some medical miracle to make me whole. It was pointless to pretend that I would wake up from this nightmare. It wasn't doing me any good to blame others or myself for what had happened. I had tried every way I could think of to deny, refuse, or ignore my fate. What I needed to know now wasn't why this had happened to me. What I needed to know was what would happen next. I felt for the first time I was ready to get busy living.

It was all just my way of looking for an explanation. Those solitary late-night sessions were bringing me back to a conviction that I had held on to since I was a kid. Back then, when my hockey star was rising, I saw it all as happening for a reason. I had been gifted with extraordinary talent for a reason. I had had a swift rise up through the ranks for a reason. I had played against the best pro teams and players and been part of the Olympics and World Championships for a reason. And that reason was Eric Le Marque. It had all been for me, by me, and about me.

But that reason wasn't enough anymore. I had lived for myself and almost died by myself. The fact that I survived must mean something, something more than I could have grasped before I lost my way on the mountain and lost my feet in the operating room. If I wasn't living for myself, what *was* I living for?

I had never been a particularly religious person. I believed in God in a general sort of way. It was hard not to when you'd seen as much of the glory of nature—the mountains at dawn and the ocean at sunset—as I had. Someone up there had put all this together. But, if anything, I just imagined a generic Great Spirit who had set the world in motion and then stepped back to let it play itself out. If you'd asked me to pin it down any more than that, I probably would have said that we're on our own, that we make our own destiny and control our own fate. After all, that's what I'd done, using my skills and abilities to reach the top rung of athletic accomplishment.

But that was gone now and I was still here. I couldn't help but wonder if maybe my life was more than just the sum of my accomplishments. Maybe all that had just been a way to bring me here, to the point of a new beginning. I've always had a natural-bred optimism. I expect things to work out for the best, and up until those eight days on Mammoth Mountain, they usually had. But the certainty I was groping for now had nothing to do with a hope-for-the-best attitude that would make sense out of the catastrophic events that had consumed me. In order to find the reason, the purpose, behind all this, it had to be real. More real than anything I'd ever experienced before.

I couldn't come up with anything more real than God. Not just the all-purpose deity who had created heaven and earth, but a specific God, who knew all about me, my strengths and weaknesses, my courage and cowardice, and, most important, the questions I asked and the answers I searched for.

It wasn't as if it all came to me in a flash of insight. God didn't reveal himself in a vision or a dream. He revealed himself through my need. Too much had happened to me, for too many reasons I didn't understand, to ever be satisfied with an explanation that didn't go beyond accidents and coincidence. If that's all it had been—if I had just stumbled onto the mountain by a simple twist of fate— then there was nothing I could learn from what I'd gone through, nothing that I could teach others. But if God had taken me up there for a reason, then it was up to me to find out what it was.

I started going to church. It was a local, nondenominational congregation near where we lived, and at first I didn't do much but sit in the back, listening and watching. Oftentimes, after a service, I'd go back to my room and get high. Like I said, God didn't overwhelm me with His reality, and for a long time, drugs had been the only reality I could tolerate. But slowly the things I was being exposed to among that community of people looking for God's purpose in their lives began to take hold and gain traction.

Nobody ever tried to get me to believe that it was God who had taken away my feet. But I heard more than once the heartfelt stories of those whose tragedies had been turned to triumph. No one ever said that I deserved what happened to me on that mountain. But I was introduced to the concept that right and wrong are real and that they carry with them the weight of their own reward. It was never revealed to me the purpose God had for making me suffer. But I came to believe that everything happens for a reason.

There were no easy answers, no simple solutions, no blind faith in a better world hereafter. But I wasn't looking for that. To tell you the truth, I wasn't sure what I was looking for or why I kept coming back.

Until I met Hope.

CHAPTER NINETEEN

Hope

MY CONNECTION WITH women has never been what you might call intimate. It might have had something to do with the role model I had growing up. After one of my first sexual encounters, with the manager of his restaurant, it was my father who reinforced the idea that women were basically objects to be used for the pleasure of men. From my early teenage years, what was normal for me more often than not involved wild parties at his house, replete with drugs and willing young women, lounging naked in the hot tub. It was a lifestyle that fit in well with the high regard I had for myself, as if I was doing any woman a favor just by letting them be seen with me. My self-absorption had precluded the kind of self-sacrificing connection that would have made for a healthy relationship, not to mention the long-term commitment of marriage.

Yet, while I took pride in my independence, I also began to feel the ache of my own isolation. For a long time I had been able to suppress that loneliness with meth, which took me so deeply inside my own head that there was no room for anyone else. It was also true that the prescription meds I was hooked on had a similar effect. For a while, I had simply existed in a remote realm of my own creation, where no one else could intrude.

But as the weeks and months wore on, and I found myself struggling to redefine the purpose and potential of my life, the faith I had in my own self-sufficiency slowly eroded. I *did* need somebody and not just to take care of me. Once I had acknowledged that I couldn't do this on my own, that my strength was simply inadequate to meet the challenges I faced, I began to yearn for connection and companionship. It had become only too clear that my perspective and point of view had come up short. I had missed out on the deeper meaning that gave life its true value. I had missed out on love.

It wasn't the love for my mother, or my family or my friends that had passed me by. I had no shortage of people who cared what happened to me and did their best to help me through. But I needed someone *I* could sacrifice for, someone who was, finally, more important to me than I was to myself. Looking back, I think that realization came from the slow saturation of spiritual truth that I was absorbing in church. The message was simple: God's intent is that we serve each other; that we lay down our lives for one another. That was the example of Jesus Christ.

I can't say that I knew how to follow that example, or

that I even tried. I was still wrestling the demons that were assailing me—anger and fear and resentment. Drugs were still blocking the flow of emotions that might have helped to heal me, if I could only have found a way to adequately express them. Being maimed had undercut the supreme confidence I once had in myself. Why, I wondered, would anyone want me now? Yet despite all those obstacles, I still had the example of Christ before me. Without even realizing it, I had taken the measure of my own lack of love. From that point on, there was no turning back.

Fortunately, I still had a bit of the old vanity that I'd always indulged in. I wanted to look nice, to present myself well and make a good impression. It was for that reason that I regularly visited a local salon to get facial treatments and a haircut. When I arrived for an appointment in the early fall of 2004, I was immediately drawn to a makeup artist and aesthetician I'd never seen there before, a woman named Hope. It helped, of course, that she was beautiful, a real knockout, but what attracted me more than anything was the spirit I sensed in her from the moment we met.

There was a gentleness, an empathy and calm center to Hope that stood in sharp contrast to the turmoil and anxiety that was haunting me. She radiated a simple unaffected strength of character that put me at ease and made me want to stay close, as if some of her qualities might rub off on me. She was warm and empathetic but I never got the impression that she lacked the hard-won knowledge of what life was really about. It was as if the hardships she had experienced had presented her with a choice: to be resentful or to count her blessings. Hope's life was full of blessings and they just naturally spilled over to those around her.

That might seem like a lot of pick up from one short encounter. Maybe it was love at first sight. All I knew was that I wanted to find out more about this person, to get close to her. Hope has a slightly different version of the story: perhaps love, not at first sight, but at first sound.

"I didn't see you when you came in," she would later tell me. "But I could hear your voice from across the room. As soon as you spoke, I got very flushed and hot and I thought, 'Whoever this guy is, I'm going to be with him. Oh my God, this is going to be my husband.'"

Hope has always been that way: attuned and aware and attentive to her own heart. It may just be a romantic myth that there is only one person in the world meant for each of us, but when I met Hope it felt like a perfect fit. She fulfilled the parts of me that had been missing for so long. Ever since that day in the salon, I've been striving to do the same for her.

In the weeks that followed our first encounter, I got to know a lot about this giving and gracious woman. My initial impression, that she had made it on her own, was amply borne out. So too was her ability to make the best of the difficulties that had come her way.

"I was born in Hollywood," she would tell me, "but when I was five, my family moved to a remote area of Minnesota. My father had stopped working in Los Angeles and decided a simpler, more satisfying life would be more beneficial for our family. We lived off the land. We built our own house, hunted and fished and farmed. The conditions were very harsh, but we never went hungry and in some ways it was a very idyllic way to live. Even though we were miles from the comforts of civilization, we learned how to be happy with very little. We were close as a family, even though my dad often had to leave for work to support us in a lean economy."

It was a confident attitude that Hope carried with her throughout her life. "When I was thirteen," she continues, "my dad got a steady job with Boeing in Seattle and we moved there. I finished high school and eventually came back down to Hollywood to start my modeling and acting career." She laughs. "I found out pretty quickly that I wasn't cut out for all the rejection, but I did discover that I had an aptitude for makeup and ultimately went to school to become an aesthetician and makeup artist. After that I started my own makeup and skin care line. I had been in a relationship that hadn't worked out and I ended up as a single mom, basically supporting my child on my own. I learned to take care of myself and my son."

I had an abiding admiration for what Hope had been able to accomplish on her own and the way that it resonated with my own independent credo. She sometimes reminded me of my own single mom, with the same mix of toughness and tenderness. But I think what really drew us together was something even more profound. We had made our own way for so long that we both felt a deep longing to share our lives with someone else. Our independence had gotten us only so far, and by the time we met and began dating, we were reaching out for a connection that had been missing too long for both of us. They say that Los Angeles—the City of Angels—is a place where people pass us by. But for me, it was the place where I found an angel. We were two lonely people who hadn't realized how alone we were until we found each other.

HOPE WASN'T MY first attempt to forge a meaningful relationship in the aftermath of my ordeal. I had briefly dated a woman who later came to visit me in the hospital. After dating her for a few months, we had a brief and unhappy marriage. The fact was, at that point I just didn't know how to connect with another human being. I agreed to marrying without really knowing what it meant, and I take full responsibility for what followed. Because of my addiction to drugs, she gave me an ultimatum: I had to choose between the drugs and her. The fact that I chose the drugs says all there is to say about my readiness to make a lasting commitment to another human being.

Then I met Hope. Did we live happily ever after? Not exactly. Finding Hope had been like discovering a key that opened the door on the possibility of a better life for me. But I still had to walk through that door, and there were many times when I resisted taking those steps, kicking and screaming all the way.

For Hope, the fact that I had lost my feet didn't seem to make the slightest bit of difference. She never once saw me as less than a whole human being and accepted my physical challenges as an integral part of who I was. After all, she hadn't known Eric Le Marque as the hockey star or the Olympic champion. I've got to say that when I let her know what I had done, she didn't seem all that impressed.

Hope, had, in fact, once seen a hockey game played by the Seattle Thunderbirds, a team that had almost re-cruited me. That would have been quite a coincidence— her in the stands, watching her future husband play. I'm not sure I would have impressed her then, either. "All they did was fight," she told me when I asked her how she liked the game. She loved me for who I was now, not who I once had been.

Of course, that person was still very much a work in progress. Going to church and meeting a wonderful woman didn't exactly work an instant transformation in my life. I was still an angry, bitter, and sometimes out-of-control drug addict. Hope immediately sensed my divided loyalties: I loved her, but I also loved the potent pills that took away all the pain and discomfort I was feeling adjusting to wearing prosthetics constantly.

With her positive influence in my life, it was as if my

heart had been divided down the middle. One half of me wanted to be with her, to give her a sense of security and provide her with the comforts that she had had to do without for some of her life. From a heavy dating schedule, we subsequently started living together and with that step also came the responsibility of being a good surrogate father to Nicholas, her son. I embraced this new accountability, seeing it as a chance to build something solid in a life that had been knocked off its foundations.

But at the same time, I resented their imposition on the isolated island that I had inhabited, like a shipwrecked survivor, for so long. Any time I wanted, I could escape to that sanctuary by chewing up a handful of pills. As the inevitable adjustments of sharing two lives began to emerge, I sought escape more and more often. The tension that my schizophrenic loyalties created only served to fuel my rage. Half the time, I wanted more than anything to be a steady and sensitive soul mate to the woman I loved. The other half, I wanted to run away and hide from the responsibility she represented, the responsibility of putting someone besides myself first. When the tension between those two extremes became too much, I exploded into fits of fury.

The breaking point came one day in April 2005 when, after a particularly bad period when it seemed as if the drugs were only giving me the sensation that my skin was on too tight, I launched into a tirade against Hope over some imagined infraction she had committed. What started as a petty display of bad temper soon escalated into full-blown violence as I pushed her around and began systemically destroying the apartment, smashing furniture and shattering dishes.

Hope may be a compassionate person, but she's never been a pushover. She wouldn't stand for the abuse and called the police. I was still busting things up when they arrived, but the sight of uniformed officers had the desired effect and I managed to get a handle on my drug-drenched emotions. Even though she declined to press charges, the cops, sensing my volatile state, weren't about to let it go at that. They ran a check on me and discovered I still had an outstanding warrant from my earlier meth possession and trespassing charge. They took me, limping and in handcuffs, to jail.

It may have been the best thing that ever happened to me. Any addict—whether their drug of choice is meth or alcohol, rage or self-pity—needs to reach a bottom before the healing process can begin. If they're lucky, they will recognize that bottom when they reach it. Otherwise, they'll find themselves revisiting it over and over again, and each time it will be worse than the last, a pit that they have dug for themselves, a personal hell they have customized to their own specifications. Los Angeles County Jail was my bottom and it would have been hard to mistake it for anything else.

With only an overworked public defender to represent me and no means to post bail, I was totally on my own. I would be incarcerated eleven days while my case slowly wound its way through the judicial system, eleven days that began with a twenty-hour check-in procedure. For nearly the entire time I was waiting to be processed, I was forced to stand, and as a result, when I was finally led to the cellblock, my amputation wounds were bleeding and showing unmistakable signs of infection. Due to chronic overcrowding, I had to share a cell with five other prisoners. We had one toilet between us. Given the raw condition of my legs, I couldn't wear my prosthetic limbs and was forced to hobble up to the bowl and climb onto it using my hands every time I needed to relieve myself. My cellmates were two crack dealers named Magic and T, an accused murderer named Anthony, a kidnapper named Pappy, and a drug-addicted Vietnam vet they called Green Eyes, who asked me to cover my legs because they were all too familiar and gruesome to look at. When I wasn't listening to them trade insults and threats, I would lie on my bunk watching the cockroaches crawling across the wall. I tried not to think about how they might be feeding on my running sores when I was asleep. I spoke to no one and jealously guarded my few possessions: one change of prison clothes, one sheet, a Bible, two pieces of paper, and a crayon. The sounds of the slamming door clashed with the echo of the wide, flat keys the guards carried, announcing their arrival for roll call and meals.

I didn't even have the advantage of a forced withdrawal during my time in jail. Because of my obvious medical condition, I was provided with Vicodin, although I was ruled out as a candidate for a bed in the jail infirmary. The problem was, I wasn't given enough drugs to maintain the high I had been accustomed to, so I spent those long hours in a nightmarish state in between being stoned and sober, craving bigger doses but denied the chance to finally flush the poison out of my system once and for all. When I was hungry, I would trade my pills for some of the food Magic had stashed under his bed. There were usually hard drugs available from the inmate trustees, and when they ran out, I quickly learned how to make moonshine with fermented fruit juice.

I made a lot of promises to myself during that time behind bars, half-crazed oaths to never let myself sink so low again alternating with vows to sue everyone in the county legal system for criminal neglect. The old patterns of rage and shame, whimpering fear and empty bravado, continued unabated. I had become, in a very real sense, an animal in a cage, reduced to my basest instincts and lashing out savagely at my captivity.

I don't remember praying to God. At that time, the idea of a loving heavenly father was just a vague concept I'd heard talked about in church. There was no way for me to make it real, not in that place, where it felt as if I had been forever forsaken and discarded. But I was wrong about that. As I said before, I think sometimes God sends His angels in human form, and when Hope came to see me in jail, it was as if she was bearing a message from the other side of those bars, a message of light and life.

"I had a hard time trying to forgive the way I was treated," she would later explain. "I had learned how to not have to depend on others, to stand up for myself and for my son. When I sensed a threat to us, I withdrew. But afterwards I thought a lot about it, what you had gone through and what you were dealing with. I tried to see things from your point of view, literally. I got down on my knees and walked around the house, trying to do all my everyday chores from that vantage. I could see how hard it was for you to cope, how high the bathroom sink was and how difficult it became just to climb into bed. I tried to lift myself. I couldn't. I tried to balance and fell every time.

"I didn't feel as if those problems excused your behavior. I honestly didn't know how much more of your anger and depression I could take. I knew the drugs were robbing you of everything, and robbing me of you. But I also realized that you weren't the kind of person who wanted to be excused. You just wanted to be understood. And I felt as if I owed that to you. Whether or not we would ever be able to make it as a couple, it was important to me that you knew I was there for you. I realized that underneath all the pain and confusion, there was a good person, someone who was trying to save himself and who deserved to be loved."

The ways of showing that love were very limited, but

Hope did the best she could. She put a hundred dollars into my jailhouse account so that I could buy food from the prison snack shop to tide me over between the inedible cafeteria food.

I won't tell you that Hope is perfect. She has her faults like everyone else. But that day she came to see me, as we talked in the visitors' booth with a pane of smudged glass between us, I knew beyond any doubt that we were meant to be together. The blows of life had broken us both, but it was through the cracks and fractures we had sustained that the light at last began to shine through, as I lay my hand through the thick bulletproof glass on hers.

I had learned enough not to expect that it was all going to be easy from that moment on. There was still a lot we had to deal with, not the least of which was all that I had gone through and all that I had put her through. But I also knew that it would now be possible to begin again.

Something was settled that day. One part of the story had ended and another was beginning. I was moving forward, slowly, haltingly, on feet that were no longer my own. The aching loss was still there. The glow from the spotlight of great achievement hadn't completely faded. There was still regret and doubt and a thousand what-ifs. But none of that really mattered anymore. What mattered was that I had hope for the future. And Hope to share it with.

CHAPTER TWENTY

Revelation

A YEAR TO the day from when I made the announcement that I would return to the snowboarding slopes, I was back on the mountain. The press, along with my family and friends, had gathered for the event. I was a little awkward, having to shimmy with a foot-long stilt to get on and off the lifts. Once I was strapped in, however, I made some great runs. I was given a new Burton by the company once my story started to come out. It didn't come close to the real Burton, the one that had saved my life, but I appreciated the gesture and it was great publicity for them. With some adjustments to my stance to accommodate my new feet, I was back, riding like before.

The sensation of gliding through fresh powder, the feeling of flying and the silence that surrounded me: it was as close to pure joy as I could come. The TV news program *Dateline* had come out to do a story on my return, and the cameraman had trouble keeping up with me.

"When I saw you on that slope," Hope later told me, "with that smile on your face, I remember thinking, 'This is what he looks like when he's truly happy.' I thanked God that you could ride again."

For a long time I had dreamed of that moment, back as far as the day they plucked me off the ridge in the Black Hawk and I had to leave Burton behind without being able to make that last, triumphant run down to Tamarack Lodge. And when I finally got back to the snow, it was everything I imagined it would be.

Almost.

The mountain hadn't changed. It was still as majestic and indomitable as ever. The thrill of floating through champagne powder was the same, too: an ecstasy unlike any other. This time, I could feel God smiling down on me. It made the snap of thin, cold air, the smell of the pine, and the invigorating wind on my face seem new again.

But something was different. I had other impressions unlike any I'd ever had before when I finally launched off those slopes for the first time in a year. The insatiable need was gone. The addiction to powder that had brought me to that place over and over again wasn't driving me any-more. I didn't need to prove that I was the best, that I was better than the mountain, or that there was no challenge that I couldn't overcome. Suddenly I didn't care about any of that. I didn't have to be the first one up or the last one off. I didn't have to have the runs all to myself or to seek out the freshest powder for my exclusive enjoyment. All that had vanished. I had been purged of that compulsive need that made snowboarding an endless pursuit of an impossible goal.

Instead, for the first time, I was simply able to enjoy myself, to let the pleasure of the moment sink in and carry me along. I wasn't chasing anything now, no ideal of athletic perfection or insatiable appetite to excel. It was fun and relaxing and that's all it needed to be. Everything I had been through since I'd last been up on the mountain had purged me of my addiction to powder. I felt clean. And more proud than I'd ever been.

The slope I was on wasn't a Double Black Diamond. It was an intermediate run, one that even a weekend rider could negotiate. But it was deeply satisfying nonetheless. I took it as it came, pacing myself, letting the journey unwind at its own speed. Along the way, I found myself thinking back on the moment by the riverbank, when I had dumped the last of my meth into the cold, clear water. I didn't know it then, but in that moment, I had made the first step in freeing myself from another addiction.

My struggle with drugs would continue, but there was no mistaking the choice that I had been confronted with that morning, when I poured out the last of the crystal meth. The decision I had made then had taken a long time to work itself into the pattern and purpose of my life, but when I thought about it, I was proud of what I had done. Meth had enslaved me and I had struck a blow for my own liberation there by the water's edge. Now, years later, taking a ride through the brilliant alpine sunlight, I could feel the chains falling away.

At the same time, the burden of my guilt and self-hatred was finally lifting. I had suffered enough for what I had allowed to happen to myself. I had acknowledged over and over my culpability and shouldered the blame for all my self-destructive behavior. Its weight had almost crushed me. But the time for recriminations was drawing to a close. How often had I told myself it would have been better for me, and everyone close to me, if I had died on that mountain? But the fact was I hadn't died. Against all odds, I had survived.

Why? I wasn't sure I knew the answer to that question. But I also wasn't sure I *needed* to know. As I slid to a stop and saw Hope coming toward me with a pleased and proud look on her face, it was enough for me just to count my blessings. More than enough.

And the blessings I was counting didn't just fall out of the sky. I didn't win the lottery or become the star of my own reality show. I had to work hard to reinvent myself and create a new set of values to live by. But what made all the difference was I didn't do it on my own. Hope was there to help. God was there to help me, providing a solid foundation of faith to build on.

After my stint in jail I began for the first time to seriously grapple with my addiction to prescription painkillers. It wasn't easy, especially because I did, in fact, have continuing medical problems that caused me a lot of discomfort. I had always been acutely aware of my body and attentive to what it took to keep it in peak condition. It was that increased sensitivity that made adjustments to my amputations all the more difficult. I could feel every little tweak and twinge that resulted from the physiological changes I was going through, changes that I had for so long masked with drugs.

But at the same time, I had a real incentive for getting clean. The ordeal behind bars had marked a definite bottom of my spiraling descent into drug dependence. Even though I would suffer more than one relapse in the months that followed, that experience had been branded deep into my brain, a harbinger of what I had to look forward to if I didn't regain control of my life. I may not have known exactly how to go about it, but there was one thing I knew without a doubt: I didn't want to go back to that place again.

In the end, I allowed Hope to decide when it was right for me to take medication. It was an act of trust that would have been previously unimaginable. Having control of my stash was the way I controlled my world. Like a chemical security blanket, it never left my side. Giving over that power was a frightening acknowledgment of my own weakness. Before that, I hadn't even been able to admit that I *had* a weakness. Now it would be up to Hope to decide when I needed relief and when I just wanted to get high, and it turned out that she had a genuine ability to discern when I was really suffering.

It's not so surprising, perhaps, that once I began to try to live drug free, I found that my tolerance for pain increased. I was able to overlook most of the aches that would before have driven me straight to the self-medicating button on my IV. Letting myself experience the full range of physical and emotional feelings was an important way to begin regaining my self-respect. I slowly stopped reacting to anything and everything and instead tried to just let it happen. I was discovering that life was comprised of good days and bad, happy times and sad, successes and failures. It was the contrasts that made it worth living.

None of these simple yet, to me, profound truths came quickly or easily. Often I would have to be taught the same lesson over and over again until it finally stuck. But I didn't beat myself up about it. I remembered the old saying from my pro hockey days: It doesn't matter how many fights you win that makes you tough, it's how many fights you're *in* that makes you tough. I was battling against a deeply engrained selfishness, a lifetime of putting myself first, and it was hardly surprising that I would revert to those old habits when the going got tough. What gave me strength in times like those was the unshakable conviction that there was no turning back.

IN OCTOBER OF 2006 Hope and I were married. A year later, we had a baby boy, Zachariah Eriq Appollos Le Marque

(ZEAL), a strapping, headstrong bruiser who totally takes after his dad. I was now a full-fledged husband and the father of two boys. It was the last thing I would ever have expected to happen. But it's turned out to be one of the best. Both my sons have been a powerful influence on me, helping me to find the strength, courage, and motivation for success I need.

If you'd asked me ten years earlier what my life would look like, I'd have had a crystal clear picture already formed in my head. I was going to be a jet-setting sports star, a hockey hall-of-famer and an Olympic champion with the world at my feet. There was no room in that equation for a wife and kids. I wasn't interested in settling down. I was destined for greatness and there was only room for one on the podium of my own ego.

But that was before. Before Mammoth Mountain. Before Grossman Burn Center. Before Los Angeles County Jail. There's a saying you hear in church circles that pretty much sums it up: Man proposes, God disposes. I proposed being a star, living for myself and taking what I wanted. God was disposed to giving me a family, teaching me to live for and serve others. It was as simple as that. I no longer felt I deserved to have my face engraved on Mount Rushmore.

Hope and I have learned a lot in church. We've heard many messages and sung a host of praise and worship songs as we've found ourselves becoming more and more a part of that family of believers. But had we heard every sermon and joined in every chorus until the end of time, it wouldn't have made any difference until we decided to apply it all to our lives. I credit that decision to sheer desperation. As I fought to get off drugs and Hope struggled with the lack of forgiveness she felt after all I had put her through, we really needed something to work for good in our lives. Without the love and acceptance and the counseling we received and the deep friendships we formed in church, I don't think we could have made it.

It wasn't about religion, about following rules and regulations or pledging allegiance to a straight and narrow lifestyle. It was about relationship. Life is based on relationships. We strengthen our lives together when we read the Bible and pray every morning and night, with each other and with our children. We fast and take communion together, making God the interwoven strength of our days. The Bible is the final word, and as for our house, we serve the Lord.

It was that serious purpose that we brought to our faith that made it real for us and bound us together in the process. We needed God and that need was what God honored.

Slowly but surely, Hope and I began to build a life for our sons and ourselves. I found a job, a great opportunity with an earthquake retrofitting company in Southern California. I have to laugh when I think about it: how a retrofitted guy found his niche in a retrofitting company. I never used to think there was honor in simple hard work.

It wasn't that I didn't strive to do my best. It was just that I always believed that my best efforts should be rewarded with the best of everything. I had no patience for the notion of an honest day's pay for an honest day's work. That was for suckers, the kind of people I used to disdain.

Now I was one of them. And I liked it. I was working a regular job, commuting to the office or the work site, looking forward to the weekend with my kids, when we tossed a ball in the backyard of the house Hope and I had bought with our hard-earned pay. The roar of the hockey crowds had faded. So, too, had the luster of Olympic glory. In their place were simpler satisfactions, everyday joys and even everyday disappointments. I was learning to appreciate what came my way, one day at a time. I learned to be grateful for what I was given, not what I could take. It was no longer about having one peak experience after another. I didn't need the rush of crystal meth or powdered snow to feel good about myself. I could look into my family's eyes and feel their arms around me and see my own worth reflected there. It is in those moments that I finally found a sense of pure satisfaction. I didn't find it in the NHL, I didn't find it in the Olympics, I didn't find it on any mountaintop, or in a bag of meth. I found it with my family.

And yet...

The old go-for-broke Eric hasn't quite ridden into the sunset yet. There are still great goals I want to accomplish, achievements to make my wife and kids, my mom and dad, proud. It goes back to the questions I get asked a lot when people hear my story: Why did all this happen to you? Was there a reason you almost died? Was there a reason you survived?

Yes, there is. I'm sure of it. So sure of it, in fact, that I want the world to know. This is why I'm currently laying plans to be the first double amputee to walk across America, from coast to coast, to help spread the message of drug abuse. I want people to know firsthand about the dangers of drugs and the consequences to all the innocent people affected. I want them to see what bad choices can mean to the rest of your life. But I also want them to see that, no matter what obstacles you face in life, it's possible to overcome, to turn tragedy to triumph.

If you never give up, you will always win. You're never defeated. That's what my grandfather used to tell me. My march across America is going to be the proof of that, echoed in every step I take. I may have lost my feet, feet that once took me down a twisted path toward a cold and desolate dead end. But sometimes you have to lose what you've got to know what you have. I was born with a resolute spirit. I was determined to do great things. The greatest thing I can do now is to use the example of my life to inspire others. To show the world you can do more with less.

You may see me walking down the streets of your town one day soon. When you do, come up and say hi. I'll be the one with no feet and a big smile.

Acknowledgments

Thank You, God, for Your salvation through Jesus Christ, Your guiding Spirit, for the second opportunity You gave me in life, and for my irreplaceable wife, Hope, who is my most cherished tangible gift from You!

Nicholas and Zachariah: Let this serve as a testimony—not of how heroic or what a survivor your dad was, but of the trickery and danger of drugs and the immediate effects they have, which can forever change your lives. Nicholas, thank you for your love of God and your understanding, intelligence, constant encouragement, motivation, and attitude. You are a champion, a world-changer, and you have a tender heart that touches all those who come in contact with you. I see you becoming an innovative producer and animator. You are my "Khabullin." Zach, thank you for your spirit, your intelligence, and your gifted athleticism. You will be a champion of God, and you will have great relationships as you become a professional athlete. In you I see myself, only times a thousand. You are my "ZEAL."

Mom: Thank you for believing in me, providing for me, and loving me when I was unlovable. Thank you for all you do for our family and for others in need, and for just being the person you are. I love you very much. Grandparents Sam and Evelyn, you will always be my inspiration and heroes. And thank you to all my other family members and friends: Without you I would be in the gutter.

John Taferner, you are a true mentor and true companion—your wisdom and guidance surpass understanding. Richard Margeson, may you be glorified in Heaven! Dad and Stella, for facilitating my rescue. In His Presence Church, Pastors Mel and Desiree, Pastors Mauricio and Virginia, Pastor Trey and Ariel Fernald, and Pastor Tim—thank you for your counsel and your leadership, and for helping us to become more like Christ. Church brothers and sisters: Thank you for your prayers, your love, and your support.

The Sherman Oaks Hospital and Grossman Burn Center: Thanks for the care, compassion, and love you provided me and my family. Kolman Prosthetics and Alex Friar: No one compares to your commitment in assisting the patients' recovery and helping them make adaptations, whatever their condition may be.

Joel Gotler, you are the best literary agent in the book business. And Davin Seay, you are hands down the best writer in the business. Thank you for your thorough understanding, incredible framing, and anointed writing. At Bantam Dell, thanks to Philip Rappaport and Brian McLendon for giving me the opportunity to share my story with the world.

Oren Koules, thank you for giving me the opportunity to embark on a life-changing endeavor. Wayne Gretzky, thank you for your support. Coaches Comley and Kyle, Northern Michigan University and Marquette, Michigan. National Guardsmen and the search-and-rescue team, for putting yourselves in harm's way to save others. Mammoth Mountain Hospital, Greg Dallas, and Mammoth Mountain, for always treating us like royalty. Cal-Quake Construction, Randy, and Simbiotica Salon. Thank you.